A GRANDMOTHER'S GUIDE TO
EXTENDED BABYSITTING

Also by Ruth Meyer Brown, M.A.
Co-authored with Margaret Dowd Connelly, M.S.

Simplified Phonics

How to Survive Parenthood
(A series of 7 booklets)

    How to Organize Your Child and Save Your Sanity

    If There's Nothing Wrong with My Child, Then What's Wrong with Him?

    How to Outwit the Sugar Monster

    Is Nutrition on Your Menu Today?

    How to Have a Party for Your Hyperactive Child and Survive

    How to Travel with Your Active Children

    How to Cope with a Chronic Bedwetter

A GRANDMOTHER'S GUIDE TO
EXTENDED BABYSITTING
Practical Advice, Inspiration, and Space for Important Information

Ruth Meyer Brown, M.A.

CAPITAL
BOOKS, INC.
Sterling, Virginia

Capital Books, Inc.
P.O. Box 605
Herndon, Virginia 20172-0605

ISBN 1-892123-70-3 (alk. paper)

Library of Congress Cataloging-in-Publication Data

Brown, Ruth Meyer.
   A grandmother's guide to extended babysitting : practical advice, inspiration, and space for important information / Ruth Meyer Brown.
   p.   cm.
  ISBN 1-892123-70-3
  1. Babysitting. 2. Grandmothers. I. Title.
  HQ769.5 .B77   2001
  649′.1′0248—dc21   2001035301

Printed in Canada

First Edition

10 9 8 7 6 5 4 3 2 1

This book is dedicated to my husband,
children,
and grandchildren.
All of them have helped to make this book possible.

CONTENTS

Chapter 1   MODERN GRANDPARENTS—WHO ARE WE?   **5**

The grandparents of today are, for the most part, well-educated, mobile, healthy, active, and ready to spend quality time with their grandchildren.

Chapter 2   GRANDMOTHER GOES BABYSITTING   **9**

Timely tips on things Grandma needs to do and think about before she departs on her babysitting adventure.

Chapter 3   SCHEDULES: GETTING ORGANIZED   **15**

Getting organized is the first step toward maintaining that warm, fuzzy Grandma image each of us imagines. Checklists for daily and weekly events, routines, and schedules.

Chapter 4   RULES MAKE LIFE RUN SMOOTHLY   **27**

Learning the family rules ahead of time lets the parents be the rule-makers, not you. Checklists cover myriad activities that can lead to disputes.

Chapter 5   CATCH THEM BEING GOOD   **37**

Positive behavior-management strategies that bring out the best in your grandchildren. An understanding and helpful approach on your part helps to create a healthy, respectful two-way relationship.

Chapter 6   FOOD: THE WAY TO A GRANDCHILD'S HEART   **47**

Planning menus with the grandchildren enhances their relationship with Grandma. Plus, information on food allergies or sensitivities that might cause headaches, stomachaches, and/or negative behaviors in your grandchild.

Chapter 7   GRANDMA'S RECIPES AND MENUS   **55**

Grandchild-chosen menus and grandchild-tested recipes that are simple to follow and easy to prepare.

Chapter 8   TIME FOR FUN   **79**

Sharing activities, outings, and special moments are all part of the babysitting experience—the part that makes it all worthwhile.

Chapter 9   ONCE UPON A TIME   **89**

You and your grandchildren can learn to use the Internet to research your family tree. But don't forget oral history, your special gift to your grandchildren.

Chapter 10   EMERGENCIES: SOS   **95**

All the information you'll need to handle most emergencies and health problems that might arise while you're babysitting your grandchildren.

Chapter 11   WHAT DO YOU MEAN I'M *HOUSE*-SITTING?   **105**

Humorous stories of actual house-sitting experiences, plus important advice and tips about how to handle house emergencies. Checklists cover essential house information.

ACKNOWLEDGMENTS

Several people have made significant contributions to this book.

My longtime friend and professional partner, Margaret Dowd Connelly, contributed to and organized my original manuscript and edited all versions of it.

My husband, Earl Brown, a writer and a computer expert, gave me full assistance with the final completion of the manuscript.

Numerous friends shared their extended babysitting adventures with me.

INTRODUCTION

WHY DID I WRITE THIS BOOK?

Teacher, parent, and author—those were my titles when I taught learning-disabled students and wrote booklets about how parents could help their children to overcome problems that were affecting their behavior both at home and at school. I've since retired from teaching, but I've added the title "grandmother" to my list, and you guessed it, I'm now writing about caring for grandchildren. But I didn't have to get another degree to learn this information. No, just a lot of years of personal experience—still the best teacher.

My saga of misadventures began innocently, with a phone call from my daughter in Minneapolis.

"Mom, could you fly up here tomorrow to babysit the children for ten days? We've had a sudden turn of events and both of us need to go on a business trip this year. We leave the day after tomorrow!"

I didn't hesitate for a moment. This was my first full year of retirement, so I had the time. And after all, I was an experienced person. This should be a lot of fun. What could possibly go wrong?

A mid-January ice storm in Virginia, twenty-degrees-below-zero weather in Minneapolis, and a two-foot accumulation of snow plagued my journey, causing me to be twelve hours late in arriving. Was my enthusiasm daunted by this omen-like series of events? No way. It was still "Grandma to the rescue!" and I looked forward to my visit with the grandchildren.

My first misstep, once I arrived, was due to a lapse in communication with my daughter. The severe weather prompted me to go to the supermarket and stock up, so I wouldn't have to take my two-year-old grandson out in the unusually cold weather. My six-year-old granddaughter gasped when she saw the large load of groceries. She opened the door to the refrigerator, saying, "Nana, where are you going to put all that food? Mom filled the refrigerator and freezer yesterday."

The misadventures continued a day later, when I missed getting the excess garbage out to the can. I was unaware that the garbage was picked up at 6 A.M. It isn't even light at that time. Oh great—overflowing garbage for another week!

A few days later the sun was shining and the weather was "warm," about twenty-seven degrees *above* zero. (It's all relative in Minnesota.) So I ventured out to do some errands. I carried the two-year-old in my arms to the car, since the snow was too deep for a stroller.

Upon returning—again with the two-year-old in my arms, plus some bags—I attempted to open the side door of the house. Oh dear, three locks! Which lock and which key—of the six keys on the key chain—would be the right combination?

In the confusion, my grandson became restless in my arms, and at that point I dropped the keys in the snow. While both my granddaughter and I searched for them, I wondered if I would be able to handle this extended babysitting assignment.

As the years progressed, I continued to have misadventures while babysitting my grandchildren. Since I only saw them twice a year, I often arrived not knowing the family rules and would even get lost on the way to the schools and the grocery store. But I learned from each and every experience. Those are the kinds of lessons that remain with you for life. Vividly.

As I talked with my friends who are also grandmothers, I learned that they were experiencing many of the same types of problems when they were babysitting. So, falling back on my teaching days as a frame of reference, I decided to write "lesson plans." I needed some goals!

(Survival sounded like a good one.) What did I need to know? (What did I need to know that I didn't yet know I needed to know?) How would I keep track of all the information I needed in order to not only survive, but to even enjoy my survival? How would I carry out my plans? And what would be my measurement of effectiveness? The last answer was easy—a happy, harmonious, and productive teaming of grandchildren and grandparents.

Those lesson plans provided the outline for this book, which I have filled in here and there with many of my own babysitting experiences. These are told as tongue-in-cheek vignettes (although a number of the stories are funny only in retrospect). Also included are some adventures of my babysitting colleagues.

For those of you who live close to your grandchildren, I hope *A Grandmother's Guide to Extended Babysitting* will be a fun read that also provides some information you might not have realized that you needed to know—particularly in an emergency.

For those of you who live a considerable distance away from your grandchildren and are only able to see them once or twice a year, I think you'll find *Extended Babysitting* definitely falls into the must-read category.

Recently I was talking with friends who do not have children or grandchildren but were planning to do some extended babysitting for friends or relatives. When I mentioned some of the areas of concern covered in this book's necessary information lists, they wanted to have a copy immediately. These friends also considered the book a must read.

For parents who employ a nanny, an au pair, or a daytime babysitter, *A Grandmother's Guide to Extended Babysitting* can also be useful. It provides a record-keeping journal that covers the essential information your child-care provider should know.

For people who provide extended babysitting for a special-needs child, this book offers numerous suggestions that will facilitate your interactions with the child. Following these tips will allow you to focus on having a fun time with the youngster.

A Grandmother's Guide to Extended Babysitting is designed to be a humorous but practical guide. It provides lists where you can record emergency information, daily and weekly routines, children's rules, suggestions on how to get organized, and information about the children's schools, their community, and housekeeping. It includes real babysitting adventures; advice about what to pack; ideas for menu planning that involve children, recipes, and cooking; and fun activities. It offers positive behavior-management strategies and food allergy/sensitivity information in the chapter called "Catch Them Being Good."

A Grandmother's Guide to Extended Babysitting aims to be an indispensable resource for all adults who care for their grandchildren—or any children—when their parents are away for several days or more and are not readily available to provide information or make decisions.

MODERN GRANDPARENTS—
WHO ARE WE?

Once upon a time it was easy to define the role of grandparents, particularly Grandma. She lived close by, perhaps next door or just down the street. You could always depend on her to have a jar of freshly baked cookies ready for you. Or perhaps she made homemade cinnamon rolls, the kind with the sweet, sticky bottoms and icing on top. As you stepped into her house in the late afternoon, the aroma of rising dough enveloped your senses. And you knew exactly where to find those tasty gems— sitting in pans on warm radiators. Like those delicious rolls, Grandma was always there for you, warm and comforting.

And Grandpa—perhaps a bit more formal in his manner—would always be there for you when you needed some help with a really important task such as fixing a flat tire on your bike or building a big project for science class. He always knew just the right way to connect all the pieces and make it work.

Other grandparents in that distant time might have lived in another town, but only an hour or two away. Your visits with them might have been less frequent, but always they were special; particularly the weeks that you spent with them during the summer ... without your parents! That was the best part. Your parents would always say, "Be sure to listen to your grandparents and pay attention to their rules."

Rules! What rules? With a sturdy bike you had free run of the local territory for as much of the day as you wanted. Of course, everyone knew who you were, so if a problem arose your grandparents would be notified immediately. (No secrets in that little town.) Dinner was always ready for you whenever you showed up in the late afternoon. Bedtime? Well, that was sometime after dark. But not until after we had all eaten homemade ice cream and cookies, while sitting on the front porch enjoying the cool of the evening. Remember that old wooden, two- person swing that hung from chains, and the wooden rocking chairs? Everyone had his favorite place to sit. What wonderful memories!

We no longer live in the era of "once upon a time." Sometimes that is good, and other times it's not so great. But we have those memories to share and also to guide us in recreating, as best as possible, memorable times for our own grandchildren.

Who are we, the grandparents of today? For the most part, we're educated, mobile, healthy, and active. To travel 2,000 miles by airplane for a brief visit with family and friends is not uncommon. Sometimes the family joke is that our children have as much difficulty keeping track of our whereabouts as they do keeping tabs on their teenagers.

For grandparents who are only able to see their grandchildren a few times a year, there are now numerous other avenues of direct communication. Not only is there the telephone, but in this computer age we have online chat rooms where we can "talk" directly to our grandchildren. No longer do we have to try to schedule phone calls at specific times; we can just leave messages through e-mail. What would *our* grandparents have thought about that?

Do we know our grandchildren any better today than our grandparents knew us? If we lived several hours drive away from our grandparents, they most likely knew as little about us as we know about our grandchildren who live a thousand miles away.

Most of the long-term extended babysitting that our grandparents did consisted of our visits to them at their homes during summer vacation or school holidays. These were relatively uncomplicated scenarios that really consisted of just that, visiting.

Today, however, parents travel extensively for business or for pleasure, and often without their children. The most obvious babysitter is—you guessed it—you. Of course, when you're asked to babysit, you say "Yes," even though the grandchildren may live several thousand miles away.

And today, whether we like it or not, the scenario is different. If the grandchildren are of school age, and the babysitting takes place during the school year, there is no choice but for the babysitter(s) to fly or drive a long distance to *their* home. And during the school year, there is nothing relaxed or laid-back about the children's daily lives.

If the grandchildren are preschoolers, often it is still easier for the babysitter to go to their home, because all their extensive equipment is there, and there is less disruption for them. (Less disruption is always good.)

So here we are—well-meaning grandparents (or other caring adults) attempting to cope with the multiple responsibilities of children, food, school, health, schedules, car-pooling, and house, and making a great effort not to feel overwhelmed.

Obviously, before we start our extended babysitting assignment, there is a lot of information we need to know. And that is what this book is all about.

2

GRANDMOTHER GOES BABYSITTING

Before setting out on my first babysitting adventure as a grandma, I fantasized about a wonderful interlude during which I'd have my grandchildren all to myself. I visualized cozy activities that would create a beautiful bond between us. The scenario resembled one of those holiday stories on TV, where the grandmother creates a marvelous atmosphere and is full of wise sayings that perfectly fit each situation.

Naturally, I wanted everything to be perfect that first time. A reasonable expectation? I thought so. Reality, however, set in soon after I arrived at my grandchildren's home.

Although my goal continues to be one of promoting a warm, cozy atmosphere, I'm now a lot wiser about how to create that scene. Some uncomfortable experiences have taught me a number of lessons that have contributed greatly to my "grandmotherly" wisdom. For example, though I would like to say "yes" to all of the grandchildren's requests, during this extended babysitting time I am actually the temporary, substitute parent. In this role, I sometimes need to say "no." And at such times the grandchildren invariably come up with something like, "But mom always lets us do it."

As part of my pre-trip planning, I now ask my daughter and son-in-law to review the rules (Chapter 4, "Rules Make Life Run Smoothly") with my grandchildren. This approach has significantly improved the atmosphere during recent trips. The parents are the rule makers, not Grandma.

At the conclusion of this last trip all of us, children and adults, were smiling and happy about our fun visit.

In order to avoid operating at a survival level, but rather on one that is comfortable, productive, and fun, your extended babysitting planning must start while you are still at home. First of all, it's important to take care of yourself. After all, we grandparents aren't as young as we were when we raised our own children. Here are some suggestions.

WHAT TO PACK

Think in terms of comfort—yours! If you're going to another part of the country, call your son or daughter for a weather update and get some suggestions about what kind of clothes to pack. Take clothing to accommodate unexpected changes in weather, too.

One year, it was eighty degrees when I left Florida, but when I arrived in Minnesota it was only thirty degrees. Then it snowed twenty-seven inches one day, and I was out front scraping snow off the sidewalk and car. Fortunately, I had been forewarned and had packed a parka and some all-weather boots.

Pack lots of comfortable clothes: sneakers, sweat suits, and even old clothes for those times when you might be cleaning or gardening. There will be occasions when you'll want to attend school functions or other special events, so pack one or two nice outfits. Don't worry about forgetting something. Wherever you're going, there will be stores. In the event you need something you didn't pack, you have the perfect excuse for buying some new clothes. It's one of my favorite excuses!

YOUR OWN CAR

It's best to have your own car whenever possible. Since my grandchildren live so far away, I always fly, but once I arrive transportation is always an issue. When the parents are busy preparing for a lengthy trip, one which involves a great deal of planning and organizing, it's almost impossible for me to use their car.

My solution to the car problem is to rent one at the airport and keep it for the duration of the trip. For me it is well worth the extra expense to have control of my own transportation. Besides, if anything goes wrong with the rental car, I can just turn it in and get a replacement.

PROTECT YOUR GOOD HEALTH

You'll probably start off your babysitting session in good health. But how long will it last? Right up until the first person sneezes on you. And that might be your very own lovable grandchild, runny nose and all. Most likely you won't have much resistance to your grandchild's germs if you are coming from another part of the country, so take special precautions. Get some of those paper masks you can buy at the drugstore! Wear one when you are in close contact with that child. Wash your hands frequently. Remember, you don't have time to be ill.

A friend recently had to go to the emergency room for a respiratory problem after she had been caring for a friend's children for a few days. She caught their illness and had to spend several days recovering. You don't have time to recover when you have full responsibility for your grandchildren for an extended period of time.

By the way, get your supply of paper masks before you leave for your trip and pack them in your carry-on bag where you can reach them in a hurry. If someone near you on the plane is sneezing or coughing, put on your mask. You don't want to share those germs with your grandchildren. They have enough of their own.

EARLY ARRIVAL

If possible, go to your son or daughter's home two or three days early, so you can learn the grandchildren's routines and complete the lists in this book before the parents depart. If you can't arrive early, make copies of the information lists in the Appendices section of this book and send them to the parents well ahead of time so they can fill in the information for you. Or just send them the book.

Soon after I arrive, I start preparing the meals and assuming my part in the grandchildren's bedtime and before-school routines. During this predeparture period, I like to do the menu planning and grocery shopping with the children, run some errands, and get ready to have the children by myself. That way there is a relatively smooth transition. This assistance is also a tremendous help to the parents—it gives them the opportunity to focus on their preparations for the trip.

ONE OR BOTH?

Unless you work well together, it's usually best for only one of the grandparents to babysit. Decide what is best for your particular situation. Personally, I like to go alone for the first week, and Grandpa likes to come the following week. This gives me a chance to get myself set in the routines and to help the parents on their way. Then for the next few days, the children and I have time to settle into our comfortable way of life.

By the second week, when Grandpa arrives, it's the start of play-time. With a second adult, we are able to do more things, and each child can have special attention. Grandpa can take one child and I can take the other. There are also things that we all do together.

A friend came up with another arrangement for two people that worked well in a long-term babysitting situation. Her health is less than robust, but she is high-spirited, enthusiastic, and good-natured. Her daughter and son-in-law had a weeklong business trip, and they needed her to care for their four children, ranging in age from less than a year to teenager. Given all the responsibility involved, this was no simple situation. But as always, my resourceful friend had a solution. Since she and the children's other grandmother are good friends, they decided to take on this extended babysitting assignment as a team. They had a great time and all went well.

SPECIAL PROJECTS

There might be special projects you can do for the family while the children are in school or taking naps. It could be mending, painting, weeding the flowers, etc. Use your imagination or just ask the parents and children if they would like to make a "Wish List" of things they'd like done while you're there babysitting. Mending happens to be my specialty; not that I do it at home, but I like to do it when babysitting. My mother always did that for me when she would visit, and I gratefully remember all the kids' clothes that got back into circulation, thanks to her.

Don't be a "fairy godmother" grandmother. It is a real temptation to do one thing after another until you have gone beyond your energy level—*way* beyond. Pace yourself and get enough rest. If you overextend yourself and don't take time for yourself, you might lose your sense of humor—and then no one will have any fun.

THINGS I WANT TO REMEMBER TO PACK

_____

_____

_____

_____

_____

_____

_____

PARENTS' AND CHILDREN'S WISH LIST

_____

_____

_____

_____

_____

_____

_____

3

SCHEDULES: GETTING ORGANIZED

In every family there are certain things that mothers and fathers do each and every day for and with their children. Over time, these activities become routines that give structure to a child's world, making him feel safe and secure.

At bedtime, for instance, there are the routines that are warm and comforting, ones that soothe the child and bring on a restful sleep. Perhaps it's a back rub, a story, a favorite toy, or a song. In addition there are the "essential" routines for all school-age children during the school year. They consist of all the schedules and deadlines involved in those before-school and after-school periods.

Learning these routines before the parents leave on their trip will contribute to the success of your extended babysitting experience. The fact that you know their routines will be a major comfort to the children—and to you in the long run. You may even begin to feel as if you really are the warm, fuzzy grandmother you envision. (Ah, Grandma—the eternal optimist!)

INFANTS' AND PRESCHOOLERS' ROUTINES

It is essential that you have the exact information about the routines of these grandchildren. In order to eliminate any confusion, the parents of the children need to write everything down for you. Be sure you know the children's warm, soothing routines also.

You must know the following specifics:

What formula to use (warm or cool) _____

When to feed the baby _____

What solid food the baby can eat _____

What the preschooler eats _____

When the preschooler eats _____

Foods *not* to give the child _____

Where the diapers are kept _____

The sleeping schedules _____

If and when baby uses a pacifier _____

Rules about infant/toddler traveling in a car _____

The location of the car seat _____

The location of the baby carriage or stroller _____

The location of jackets/sweaters/hats _____

MEALTIMES

Meal preparation and cleanup can be tedious if you are alone in the kitchen doing all the work. Learn what kitchen duties the older grandchildren have so they can help. If you have planned the meals with them, they will often be there with you doing the stirring and measuring. They can be part of the "management team" when you are babysitting, and help prepare the foods of their choice.

You can eat dinner at a table or in front of a TV. Dinner around a table, with the family sharing stories about what happened during the day, can be wonderful. My grandchildren like the special ambience created by a combination of soft lights, candles, and flowers. This, along with the food of their choice, makes for a most pleasant meal.

Mealtime Chores

Who helps prepare the meal? _____

Who sets the table? _____

How is the table cleared of dirty dishes? _____

Who washes dishes or loads the dishwasher? _____

Who empties the dishwasher? _____

Who puts out the garbage? _____

Who does other kitchen-related jobs? _____

Other Mealtime Chores

_____

_____

_____

_____

_____

_____

MORNINGS

Not knowing the daily schedule when you are babysitting causes a great deal of anxiety for all concerned. The before-school preparation, for instance, can be a real ordeal if you don't know the morning routines. The first few days I'm alone with the children, the process of getting them off to school—clothed, fed, with lunches packed, important papers signed, books and homework in backpacks, and on time—tends to turn me into a "nervous grandma." I get a bit hyper and overly conscious of children dawdling at breakfast. (My daughter describes it as having my "worry button" punched on HIGH.) Once I am familiar with the routine and am well-prepared, I relax—somewhat.

If you have fixed yourself a delicious cup of coffee or tea and plan to enjoy it while the children are getting ready for school—save it! Wait until *after* they leave, since it will just get cold while you are rushing around.

After living for a number of years in an "adults-only house" (just Grandpa and Grandma), where breakfast is leisurely and quiet and there is undisturbed time to read the entire newspaper, breakfast with the grandchildren can be an assault on your senses. Be prepared.

A.M. Routines

You need to know the following information:

Wake-up time _____

Dressing routines (Does anyone need help with clothes or hair?)
_____

Breakfast time _____

Who packs lunches? _____

Lunch money amount _____

Departure times _____

School bus schedule _____

Bus numbers _____

Additional reminders _____
_____
_____
_____
_____

Note: Grandma's routine is to check that lunch boxes are next to backpacks.

AFTERNOONS

Part of *your* afternoon routine should be to take a nap, if at all possible. It is such a temptation to keep doing one household chore or errand after another. Give yourself a break. Take a walk if there are no napping preschoolers, read a book, knit, exercise, play computer games, write letters or e-mail friends—do something relaxing for yourself.

Afternoons with preschoolers can be busy, but afternoons with school-age grandchildren are even busier. The period from after school until bedtime can pose a number of challenges, too. The children may arrive home tired, hungry, happy, angry, sad, late for some sort of practice, or . . . take your pick. For you, there is often driving involved. One of the children may accidentally miss the school bus or may be asked to stay after school to help paint the scenery for a play. This means, of course, that you will have to do a pick-up at the school, either immediately or when the child is through painting scenery. You might also be responsible for chauffeuring the children to and from their various after-school activities, including athletic practice/games, rehearsals, dance/music lessons, scout meetings, etc. And don't forget, there is still homework to do.

For these reasons I always keep some sort of food in the freezer or refrigerator that can be a quick fix for dinner. I call it "flexible food"— something either leftover or instant, but still part of the menu created by the children. You might have planned a meal that takes a fair amount of prep time, but when there is a change of plans and you suddenly have a lot of added responsibilities with the children, fix the "flexible food."

List some "flexible foods" you like to fix:

_____

_____

_____

_____

_____

_____

_____

_____

_____

Afternoon Routines

Schedules and routines that you need to know:

After-school arrival home _____

_____

Where do the books and homework go? _____

After-school activities (times and places) _____
_____
_____

Homework (time and place) _____
Dinnertime _____
Chore times _____
_____

Somewhere around dinnertime you and the children need to decide what they would like for breakfast. The children also should help to organize their lunches for the next day by bringing their lunch boxes to the kitchen and cleaning out the leftover debris. The ice blocks need to be put in the freezer, and the lunch boxes should be packed that evening with the nonperishables. Have the children tell you what they want for lunch the next day, so you don't have to think about it in the morning. (Smart grandmas write this information down.) If the children buy lunch, they should put the lunch money in their backpacks after dinner.

BEDTIME

"Icing on the cake"—that's what I call bedtime back rubs, songs, stories read and stories told. If the children want all this "icing," they need to follow through in a pleasant and timely manner with their bedtime preparations.

Bedtime Routines

Nightly checklist:

Pack books and homework in backpacks _____
Place the backpacks next to the exit door _____
Place hat, jackets, boots, sweaters, umbrellas (as needed) next to exit door _____
Lay out clothes for next day _____

Bath time _____

Who needs help with the bath? _____

Who does the hair washing? _____

Brush teeth _____

Put on pajamas _____

"Icing on the cake" details:

What do the children like best (back rubs, songs, stories read, hugs, kisses, etc.)? _____

Describe other bedtime routines _____

_____

_____

PETS

When I babysit my grandchildren, the care of pets is not really an issue. They have a friendly, well-trained cat that sleeps in its own place and doesn't bother things around the house. The children feed it and take care of the litter box.

During my last trip, however, a small tree frog also was under my care. The children had discovered this creature hopping around in the upper hall. It was winter, and they speculated that it must have come in with their potted plants sometime in the fall. Now, because it was warm, the frog was finished hibernating and looking for food and water. They bought the perfect container and thought they had met all its needs—all except for food.

Tree frog food ... let's see now, what does a tree frog eat? Live grasshoppers, of course. (Doesn't everyone know that?) But in Minnesota in early March, you can't even find a grasshopper outside—much less catch one—which probably explains why most tree frogs were still quietly hibernating in anticipation of spring. In order to buy the live grasshoppers we needed to feed this frog (so he wouldn't expire on my watch), I made the thirty-minute drive to a specialty shop. Once there, the question was, "What size grasshoppers?" Size? They come in sizes? I bought the large ones.

Finally back at the house, I dumped the grasshoppers into the frog's container (one got loose, but the cat took care of that one) and the frog gulped the first one he could reach. I realized my mistake right away. I should have gotten the smaller grasshoppers. The legs of the grasshopper were left hanging out of the frog's mouth for quite a while. It wasn't a pretty sight.

Of course the grasshoppers needed food too, so I had to keep a few slices of fresh potatoes in the container for the grasshoppers to eat! In addition, crumpled paper towels were kept in the container to provide hiding places for the grasshoppers. The frog occupied the rock structures and perched on the side of the water container. Actually the tree frog is quite an interesting little creature and chirps in the evening. I learned a lot on that trip.

I've heard a variety of pet stories from friends that might be of interest to any adult volunteering to do extended babysitting. In many situations the grandchildren were just fine—it was the pets that turned out to be a number one bother.

Various stories included very spoiled pets that believe they are people, sleep with the adults and refuse to settle down elsewhere, and bark/meow a lot when they don't get what they want. There are other stories of large, friendly dogs who are a lot of fun to have around, but who are prone to snatching food off the table if the food and the dog are left unattended. Some cats also have been known to eat food that is ready for the family, given the opportunity.

Some people and their pets are very attached to each other, which is just great. However, the babysitting adults might not have the same interest in those pets, and it could be asking a bit too much of them to take responsibility for these demanding animals in addition to the children.

In certain cases, my friends will insist that other arrangements for the pet be made before they agree to babysit again. It might be that the offending animal needs to be housed elsewhere while the parents are away. The pet could be placed in a kennel or stay with friends of the parents, or the parents could take the "difficult" pet with them on their trip.

When you are getting ready for an extended babysitting stint, it is fair to ask the parents about the habits of the pets—and even to ask that the pets be housed elsewhere if there seems to be a potential problem.

Pet Particulars

If there's a pet in the picture, this is the information you need to know:

Who feeds the pet(s)? _____

Who walks the dog? _____

Where is the leash kept? _____

Who changes the cat's litter box? _____ How often? _____

Where does the pet sleep? _____

May the pet be outside? _____

Other duties, details, and routines: _____
_____

Your Favorite Outrageous Pet Story

_____
_____
_____

LAUNDRY

In some families, older children are already independent about doing their own laundry. The younger grandchildren, of course, need their clothes to be washed and dried for them. Sorting my grandchildren's socks, underclothes, and T-shirts, however, can be a big mystery. I'm never sure who owns what. The answer is to have a "sorting-folding-let's-put-the-clothes-away" party. It works every time. That way the children are sure their favorite shirts will be put back in their own drawers.

One of my favorite laundry stories is one a friend told me about the time she was babysitting her four-year-old granddaughter. My friend had several things she wanted to iron. After searching for an ironing board and iron for some time, she finally came upon the two in the back of a hall closet. She set everything up and began to iron. The four-year-old came into the room and just stood there staring at her grandmother.

Then the little girl walked around to the other side of the ironing board and just watched her iron.

After a while the child asked in a puzzled voice, "What are you doing, Grandma?"

"I'm ironing, dear."

"What does it do?"

"It takes the wrinkles out of the clothes."

"Why do you do that?"

My friend was just as puzzled as her granddaughter. It took her a few seconds to grasp the situation. And then she began to wonder herself why she ironed. Talk about a generation gap. With everything so wrinkle-free these days, the child had no experience with such things as an iron and ironing board. "No wonder it took me so long to find the darn things!" my friend said.

The Dirt on the Laundry

Laundry information you probably should know:

Where is the dirty laundry basket kept? _____

Is each child responsible for putting his dirty laundry in that basket? _____

Which children do their own laundry and when? _____

Any special operating instructions for the washer and/or dryer?

_____

When can we have the clothes-folding party? _____

Is ironing expected? _____

Other laundry and clothes instructions: _____

_____

_____

CALENDAR

Think how busy parents are, keeping up with the daily, weekly, and monthly schedules for their children. Think how frenzied you would be if you, the babysitter for the next few weeks, didn't know all these schedules. Just the thought makes me weak in the knees—and possibly a bit nauseated!

A large calendar in my daughter's kitchen usually contains all the important, scheduled information. Once I've checked her calendar of events, I write each one in a notebook along with such specific information as time, location/exact address, and the directions on how to get there. This covers meetings, practices, performances, games, and whatever else might be on the grandchildren's agenda.

"Picky, picky," some might say about all the schedules and lists. But if you are able to master the family's schedule, life can be quite pleasant, even fun. What's *not* fun is turning into a Grinch-like person because you can't get a handle on things and you begin to feel out of control.

When you don't have to worry about who's going where and when, you can enjoy the big things and not sweat the small stuff.

Grandma's Planner

Scheduled events you should know about:

Athletic practice/events _____

_____

Other activities/events _____

_____

Scout meetings _____

_____

Weekly appointments for physical/speech therapy _____

_____

Doctor appointments _____

Dentist appointments _____

Orthodontist appointments _____

Other appointments _____

_____

_____

GRANDMA'S MAILBOX

How are you going to deal with:

Field trip permission slips to be signed?
A note from a teacher requiring your signature?
Homework/test papers to be signed?
Other important mystery papers that need your attention?
Phone or other messages?

A friend of mine had an outstanding answer to this question. She calls it "Grandma's Mailbox." She places a box in the kitchen where the children can put papers requiring her attention.

ORGANIZED: THAT'S ME

Feeling overwhelmed when you consider all the details you must deal with when you have full responsibility for the children? Want to reconsider that generous extended-babysitting offer you made to your son or daughter? Never fear! Your time with the children will be a fun, productive event because, with this book in hand, you will be well prepared.

You might also want to check out a booklet called *How to Organize Your Child and Save Your Sanity,* by Ruth Brown and Margaret Connelly (Cottage Park Publications, 1999). It may be ordered directly from the publisher: Cottage Park Publications, PO Box 1583, Vienna, VA 22183-1583. The price is $4. Please include a check with your order.

4

RULES MAKE LIFE RUN SMOOTHLY

Are family rules written in cement? Carved in stone? Perhaps not. But before your babysitting assignment begins, the rules regarding certain issues need to be discussed in a meeting with the grandchildren, parents, and grandparents all present. Some rules may even need to be put in writing.

The issue of rules can be the most difficult part of extended babysitting, particularly when the grandchildren are pre-teens and teenagers. A natural part of their development is the desire to have more freedom and to make their own decisions. And at times they tend to push the limits.

During one visit with my grandchildren, there were a few situations that required immediate long-distance phone calls to their parents in order to clarify an issue. If rules had been discussed before the parents left, that visit would have been more harmonious.

The guidelines that follow may seem rather firm and direct, but dealing with these issues ahead of time actually allows you to be more relaxed and to enjoy some very pleasant times with your grandchildren. Let the parents be the rule makers, allowing you to be the warm, fuzzy grandparent that you'd like to be.

The ages of the children, of course, determine the need for various rules. Social issues tend to be an area of contention with children from late grade school on. This topic can be a difficult one for the parents to handle as well.

After considering the myriad activities that can lead to disputes, I've identified the following major areas of potential conflicts:

Friends
Sleepovers
Nighttime activities
Clothes
Telephone
Homework
Television
Computers
Allowance
Chores
Athletic equipment
Parks and playgrounds

FRIENDS

Here are issues that should be addressed:

When are the children allowed to socialize with friends? _____

Which friends are okay for them to socialize with? _____

Friend's phone _____ address _____

Friend's phone _____ address _____

Any friend on the "NO" list? _____

"NO" list friend's phone _____ address _____

Whose house is off-limits? _____

Is the child allowed to go "mall walking" with friends? _____

Does the teenager have permission to drive in the parent's absence? _____

Can he/she ride with other teen drivers? _____

Is there a curfew on school nights or weekends? ___ Time? ___

Are dates allowed? What are rules concerning dates? _____

What places are the children not allowed to visit? _____

SLEEPOVERS

Is your grandchild allowed to go on sleepovers while you are in charge? If it's not one that has been preplanned and approved by the parents—like a friend's birthday party—I always say "no" to them when I'm babysitting. I think "sleepovers" or "slumber parties" are misnomers because no one ever sleeps at them, and the kids are always cranky the next day. Their crankiness can spoil any special activities you may have planned for that day, and it tends to flow over to other siblings, creating unpleasant situations.

The rules for sleepovers:

Are they allowed? No _____ Yes _____

At grandchildren's house? No _____ Yes _____

At friend's house? No _____ Yes _____

Is one planned at a friend's house during my visit? _____

Friend's name _____ phone _____

Address/directions _____

_____

Date/time of sleepover _____

What else do I need to know? _____

_____

_____

NIGHTTIME ACTIVITIES

Before the parents depart, ask them: Are there any nighttime special events that involve driving a child somewhere in the early evening and then picking him or her up later on? This seems simple enough, but there might be a younger sibling who will be sleeping by pickup time. The younger child can't be left alone and would be better off if not disturbed. Also, you may have concerns about driving alone in a strange city at night. When I'm babysitting by myself, I say "no" to any such evening activity (which never wins me any points with my grandchild).

With teens there are almost always scheduled practices, games, and concerts that are required if they are part of a team or group. Ask the parents of the children to arrange alternative transportation during the time of your visit.

Essential nighttime activities: _____

_____

Possible nighttime activities: _____

_____

Nighttime activities on the "NO" list: _____

_____

_____

CLOTHES

Clothes are another area where children push the limits. When your grandchild dresses for school in apparel that is too tight, too revealing, too whatever—and it's almost time for the school bus—it's too late to have a discussion about appropriate clothing. That's why you need to work this out ahead of time—before the parents leave and you're on your own.

Clothes that may *not* be worn to school:

_____

_____

_____

TELEPHONE

The hours that a child can spend on the phone, if left unsupervised! (Although more and more kids are communicating on the Internet these days.) Again, this is an issue that needs to be discussed while the parents are still home.

Rules for phone use:

When _____

How long _____

Does the teen have a cell phone? What is the number? _____

Times when phone can't be used? _____

Other phone restrictions _____

TELEVISION

Learn the parental rules for television, including:

How often may children watch TV? _____

How long? _____

When? _____

What programs are allowed? _____

What programs are not allowed? _____

Which channels are allowed? _____

Which ones are forbidden? _____

How close can they sit? _____

HOMEWORK

Ask the parents how they handle homework. Before they leave, discuss study time, when and where it takes place, and the routines. Discuss what activities must wait until homework is done.

I pay close attention to all homework, teaching whatever the child is having trouble learning. Sometimes if she has gotten way behind on homework, I spend time helping her catch up. Also, I always help the grandchildren start, and—hopefully—finish all long-term projects. That helps to ease school tension for the parents as well as the children.

The rules for homework:

When _____

Where _____

How long _____

Music, TV, phone calls allowed during homework time?

Yes _____ No _____

COMPUTERS

In this computer age the concerns are:

Is there a computer designated for parents only that is not to be used by the children? _____

Where? _____

Is there a computer for the grandchildren to use? _____

Where? _____

When may the children use the computer? _____

For how long? _____

What software applications/programs are they allowed to use? __

_____

What software applications/programs aren't they allowed to use?

_____

Are they allowed to go on the Internet? _____

What are their limitations regarding Internet surfing? _____

Other information: _____

_____

ALLOWANCE

A child's allowance is an important issue. Often the money is linked to chores and responsibilities. If you are going to be responsible for giving it out, be clear about the amount each child is given, any requirements he or she must fulfill, and when it is paid. Also have an understanding about how the children are allowed to spend the money.

One time, the grandson of a friend of mine talked her into taking him to the local hobby shop where he proceeded to spend more than $30 on Pokemon cards, telling her all the while that his mom lets him "___ spend my allowance money any way I want." His mom let my friend know differently when she returned home! "YOU DID WHAT?? THIRTY DOLLARS??" was her response when my friend told her about the hobby shop excursion and the world of Pokemon cards.

Allowances for each child:

Child _____ amount _____

Child _____ amount _____

Child _____ amount _____

Child _____ amount _____

When paid? _____

Requirements/stipulations _____

Spending restrictions? _____

GRANDCHILDREN'S CHORE LIST

Hopefully, the parents have left a chore list so that you'll know which household jobs each child is responsible for. If not, you could just make a general chore list similar to the one below.

Name _____

Chores _____

_____

_____

Name _____

Chores _____

_____

Name _____

Chores _____

_____

Name _____

Chores _____

_____

ATHLETIC EQUIPMENT

Even though the older grandchildren should be responsible for knowing where their athletic equipment is, you should learn where the various pieces are supposed to be kept. Then you can have the children put the equipment back after using it. Knowing where equipment is stored will also make hunting for bicycle helmets, shin guards, that favorite bat, ball and glove, etc., a lot less painful. I like to go bike riding with the grandchildren, but if I need a tire pump and can't locate it, we all miss out on an opportunity for a fun outing.

Locations for storing athletic equipment:

Bikes _____ Bike tire pump _____

Helmets _____ Shin guards _____

Baseball bat, ball, glove _____

Football _____ Basketball _____ Soccer ball _____

Inline skates _____

Ice skates _____ Hockey stick, puck _____

Skis, poles _____ Boots _____

Snowboard _____ Boots _____

Bathing suits _____ Surfboard _____

Boogie board _____ Snorkel, fins, goggles _____

Other _____

Sports Rules:

Where can the children skate or ride bikes? _____

Can they go alone? _____

Do they need supervision or assistance with:

Biking? _____

Skating? _____

Swimming? _____

PARKS AND PLAYGROUNDS

Know where the parks and playgrounds are. It is fun to take the younger grandchildren there to play on the equipment. If it is warm, there might be a wading pool, and splashing around in that is always lots of fun. Usually there are other children for your grandchildren to play with.

If the grandchildren are older (grade-school age) find out the family rules regarding parks and playgrounds.

May they walk there? _____

May they ride their bikes there? _____

Do you need to drive them? _____

Park _____

Location/directions _____

_____

Playground _____

Location/directions _____

_____

If scheduled practices and games for the grade-school children and the teenagers are held at parks and playgrounds, and you are the one driving them to and from these practices and games, it is essential that you locate these places on a map. Keep that map in the car.

CARVED IN STONE = WARM AND FUZZY

Is it possible to have a connection between these two descriptions? Of course! The parents make the rules (carved in stone), leaving you the freedom to be the warm, fuzzy grandmother.

That is still my goal. I have learned from years of babysitting grandchildren—as well as years of raising children and teaching—that if sensible, safe rules are understood and followed by the children, they provide a framework for relaxing and enjoying my time with them. And this framework needs to be established by the parents *before* they leave on their trip.

5

CATCH THEM BEING GOOD

When I am babysitting my grandchildren for a week or two, I don't want to be thought of as the Wicked Witch of the West—but I do try to keep some sort of order. As you know, even with the best of plans and intentions, there are times when things get out of control. I have learned—sometimes belatedly—some very helpful strategies.

One of the best strategies I have used is called "Catch Them Being Good." It's simple and only takes a few seconds of your time. It works well because children always respond positively to sincere praise. Think of how you would have responded to the following when you were a child:

"I like the way you did that."

"You really finished that job fast!"

"Your room looks lovely since you cleaned it!"

"Your toys look great when all the cars are lined up like that on the shelf."

"Thank you for helping your brother clear the table."

Some children use a tactic that is most frustrating to the adults. It is really a game of control, and the child plays it by quietly doing nothing.

For instance, in the morning, when there is a tight schedule for getting up, getting dressed, eating breakfast, and being ready for school, this child will be in his bedroom, in bed or playing with toys, but definitely not getting ready for school. Eventually he misses the bus—meaning you will have to drive him to school. You are fuming, either quietly or otherwise, and you start to wonder why you ever volunteered for this job. A rapid count reminds you that you still have seven days until Mom and Dad return. Groan!!!

THE STAR SYSTEM

If you are caring for children in preschool through early elementary school, this is the perfect time to establish a star chart and take a more organized approach to "Catch Them Being Good." Make a chart on a large sheet of paper, listing the days of the week across the top. Down the left side list the A.M. activities the child is passively not doing, but print them in a positive manner.

For example:

	Monday	Tuesday	Wednesday	Thursday	Friday
Get up on time	_____	_____	_____	_____	_____
Get dressed on time	_____	_____	_____	_____	_____
Eat breakfast on time	_____	_____	_____	_____	_____
Leave for school on time	_____	_____	_____	_____	_____

A chart like this can be used for the five school days or all seven days if there are weekend schedules to keep.

Explain to the child that every day he will earn a star for each of the listed activities—if he does it on time. Be sure to mark a star as soon as the child has done each task and congratulate him on it. (I just use a red pen to put the stars on the chart). Once the child has earned a star, he never loses it.

There are different ways of counting the stars for a reward. If there are four activities on the chart, in five days the child could earn a total of twenty stars. When a child has earned a certain number of stars (say, for instance, he has gotten dressed right away for five days in a row), he can have a special treat. Or perhaps if the child has earned a total of fifteen of the possible twenty stars in a week, there might be a treat. The rewards shouldn't be big or expensive—perhaps an extra TV program, an extra story read, an extra trip to the library, his choice of dinner that night, his choice of dessert, etc.

The important thing is to reward the improvement and to be complimentary about it. The problem won't be solved immediately, and things may be moving more slowly than you might like, but improvement is always progress.

A number of stores have great stickers. One kind that my daughter used for a star chart was a large colored rainbow. If, at the end of the week, the child had a perfect row of stars, even just for one task, he or she got a rainbow. The child was always happy to put that special sticker at the end of the perfect row and count how many rainbows he had earned that week.

With this approach, the focus is on the positive, and soon you will see improvement in the child's behavior. All too often adults are quick to respond to a child's negative behavior, but that approach can result in confrontations that really don't improve matters and put a strain on the relationship. If you find yourself doing this, it's time to change your approach by responding to and rewarding positive behavior. Try "Catch Them Being Good." You'll love it!!

A note of caution: Since getting ready for school sometimes makes children anxious, you must be careful not to fuss at them with statements such as:

"If you don't hurry I won't give you a star," or

"Come on, come on, you're going to miss the bus."

Just say nothing, except maybe to talk about pleasant things and to compliment the child for what he or she is doing. Give a red star for any of the activities that are done on time.

A child's passive behavior is a learned behavior, a game that the child has learned to play over a number of years. But, using patience, warmth, kindness, and understanding, you can help the child change do-nothing, passively controlling behavior to a more positive, constructive way of doing things.

How did I learn this star chart approach? Painfully! In my first year as a resource teacher for learning disabled children, I had a group of eight second-grade students, mostly very active boys, who were supposed to come across the hall to my classroom. They had a lively, rough-and-tumble time along the way, even with me standing at the hall door supervising. When they finally entered my classroom, they didn't go near their seats, much less get ready for instruction with their crayons and pencils at hand.

A wonderful, wise school psychologist taught me how to use a star chart. The requirements in the beginning were minimal: walk quietly across the hall, sit in your assigned seat, have writing materials with you, and be quiet—in other words, be ready for instruction. The first day I had my doubts as I stood at the star chart waiting for even one student to do something to earn a star.

Gradually, though, they drifted toward their assigned seats and were pleased to learn they could earn a star for each one of those "easy things." Within three days, all of the students were coming to class in a lovely, cooperative manner. Once they were comfortable with the arrival routine, I changed the star chart to reflect such academic behaviors as listening, taking turns and not calling out answers, raising their hands if they had a question, etc. The children progressed in the ensuing months to becoming delightful, cooperative students. I thoroughly enjoyed knowing and teaching them, and I think that we all learned a lot from each other.

OTHER POSITIVE APPROACHES

Does the same star chart have to be used forever? No. As the child's behavior changes and improves, new jobs and activities can be listed as needed. The point of the star chart is to teach children positive behaviors that assist them in becoming dependable and independent. When that happens, they no longer need a star chart; just our verbal praise and interest will be sufficiently rewarding to them.

When an older grandchild (upper grade school to grade twelve) is dragging in the mornings, talk with him or her and see if there is something wrong. Is there a school paper overdue? Is there a special breakfast he would like? How well did she sleep? Does he have a headache or temperature? Did she go to bed too late? Are there no clean clothes to wear? How can you help him or her feel better in the morning? He or she will appreciate your empathy.

An understanding and helpful approach on your part helps to create a healthy, respectful two-way relationship with your older grandchild. I used that strategy with my upper-grade-school students with great success. Some children are resistant to authority figures, whether at school or home. But when the authority figure respects them and treats them as thinking individuals—and makes a point of catching them being good—then positive, self-disciplined behavior develops.

It was so much fun to watch my students progress through the stages towards self-disciplined behavior. As they would catch themselves doing something wrong and change independently to a positive behavior, quite often they would look up to see if I had noticed. We wouldn't say anything; we would just smile at each other.

Some children have a sense of maturity and responsibility even as young children that helps them to be very independent. Other children need help learning these skills. But these skills are essential for each individual to learn. Our job as adults is to have the patience to give each child the help he or she needs.

When a child has a chore to do and is very slow in doing it, it also helps if you offer assistance in a good-natured way. Don't scold, just make the task easier to accomplish. Quite often I'll say, "Let's finish this together in a hurry. Then we can play a game (or read, or go for a bike ride, etc.)." It takes the emphasis off the task and the negative feelings that she might be feeling. At a later time, the child will often be more cooperative about her chores.

Sorting clean clothes is something I always do with my grandchildren. First, because I'm not always sure which socks and shirts belong to which child, and second, because it makes the endless task go much faster. We have a "clothes-folding get-together." Actually, it's often a fun time when we're sitting and folding and talking together. As soon as the clothes are folded, the children take them to their bedrooms and put them away. (That's one step beyond just getting the clothes through the bedroom door and left on the bed or a chair.)

Another successful strategy is to maintain the schedules and routines that the parents have established. Meal and bedtime schedules are the most important ones to keep. When either of those run late, children tend to become cranky and difficult.

FOOD AND BEHAVIOR

I've always found food to be the biggest area of contention—or contentment—when it comes to interacting with children. There are advertisements everywhere showing grandparents taking their grandchildren for an outing and feeding them all kinds of junk food full of sugar and artificial coloring. That might do for a special day, particularly when the grandparents are giving the children back to the parents by nighttime. But if you have the children for two weeks and you take them out for a day that includes lots of junk food, you will pay for it.

As a military wife who often traveled and moved with young children, I learned that provisioning healthy food (always available in the cooler in the car) was the key to having successful, happy trips. From those earlier experiences, I've learned to always pack snacks and/or lunches for my grandchildren whenever we are going for an outing, whether it's for just two hours or for the whole day. That way the children can eat when they get hungry, instead of waiting until you can find some food to buy.

One snack that works well for my grandchildren is apple slices. I like to put them in separate plastic sandwich bags, one for each child to carry in a pocket. Another great snack is popcorn, and I pack that in individual baggies also, in order to eliminate arguments about who ate more than the other. (A note of caution: Be aware that popcorn is considered a choking hazard for kids under three.) And individual bottles of water are essential. We save the smaller plastic water bottles, refill them with water, freeze them, and then everyone carries his own. That way each child can snack when he or she feels hungry or thirsty.

When my grandchildren and I are ready to rest, we find a comfortable place and eat our picnic lunch. That way, the bulk of the food they eat is sensible and doesn't upset their systems. Afterwards we might have a treat such as ice cream or cookies, or some other specialty we find on the way.

I experienced the effects of sugar overload once when my son was three years old. I was living with my parents for a year while my husband was stationed overseas. My son was very healthy, with a great appetite. But for that last month he became fussy and wouldn't eat. My mother, dad, and I just couldn't understand what was causing this.

Finally my husband came home and we were saying goodbye to the neighbors. One neighbor said how much my son had enjoyed that dish of homemade ice cream she had given him every day. Another said he had enjoyed the homemade cookies she had given him every day, and a third neighbor remarked that my son really liked those little chocolates she had given him every day.

All of these lovely, gentle neighbors had thoroughly enjoyed my son during the year, and liked sharing these treats with him that last month. But that excess sugar created havoc with his appetite. I didn't say anything to those dear people, because we were moving away from that area, and they meant well. And my son's appetite and disposition returned to normal once the excess sugar was eliminated from his diet.

Some of the best extended babysitting experiences my children had while they were growing up were with my parents. My parents were sensible, calm, very attentive in a warm, fun way, and they always maintained their grandchildren's eating and sleeping schedules. Yes, there were desserts, since Mother was a superb chef, but those sweet things were eaten after a meal and not snacked on indiscriminately all day.

ORGANIZATION IS EVERYTHING

If you do not have children living at home, it is fairly easy to keep yourself organized and on schedule—even if occasionally you have to rush and catch up after waking up late in the morning. With children it doesn't work that way. You need to be constantly thinking, planning, and organizing ahead of time. You need to be super-organized!

A friend of mine does some extended babysitting that takes my breath away, as experienced as I am. Just recently she was babysitting four of her grandchildren. You might think that doesn't sound so difficult. But these grandchildren were four-year-old quadruplets.

I asked her how she handled the morning activities—getting four preschoolers dressed and fed seemed like an overwhelming task. Not a problem. She went right downstairs to make breakfast, and when the four came down they had already dressed themselves and were ready to eat. Obviously the parents had done a superb job of teaching the children self-help skills; however, my friend still had to be sure that their clothes were clean, ready to wear, and laid out every night, just as the parents did. Stick to the routine, be organized, and things will go well—most of the time.

My friend also likes to take the quads for an outing every day, but she never does it alone. She hires an adult babysitter for a period of time each day, and the two adults can safely do a lot of fun activities with the four children.

Now that my grandchildren are grade-school age and older, I always plan outings with them and prepare for the excursion the night before. Included in the planning process is agreeing on the time we will all be up for breakfast and the time we plan to leave the house. Some children (especially teenagers) really like to sleep late on weekends or during summer vacation, while their siblings are ready to leave the house in the early morning. This discrepancy can be a major source of bickering, so it must be discussed and resolved the night before.

BEDTIME, BICKERING, AND OTHER COMMON PROBLEMS

Sometimes no matter how organized or pleasant and accommodating we are, things just don't go well. For instance, sometimes children (often grade-school age) really push the limits and just refuse to go to bed. A friend tried this effective strategy. She had spent a pleasant evening with the children: leisurely baths, stories, talking, etc. But it was a school night, and the children were being as resistant to bedtime as they had been for the last three nights. By 9:30 P.M. my friend became disgusted with the "game playing," went into her bedroom, closed the door, and went to bed to read. Immediately the children were in her room asking her to tuck them in bed. She stayed firm and said no, they would have to put themselves to bed that night, since she wasn't going to put up with them fussing and arguing about bedtime. It worked! After that, the children were very cooperative and pleasant at bedtime.

Another friend has different concerns when she cares for her older grandchildren. "It was so easy to babysit the grandchildren when they were preschoolers," she says. "When I wanted to take them out for a while, I could just put them in the car and go." The worry now is that her oldest grandchild is sixteen and has a driver's license. This creates a whole new area of potential problems. Specific rules are needed— rules established by the parents and clear to both the teenager and the babysitter.

Bickering among siblings drives me crazy. Quite often it has to do with space and getting into each other's territory. When my grand-children were watching TV, they fussed about where each one was—or wanted to be. I decided to assign a seat to each child. I called the oldest child into the living room and gave that child the choice of four different places to sit. She chose a certain chair as her assigned seat. I called the second child into the room and gave him a choice of the remaining three seats. He chose the couch. From then until I went home, the children had their assigned TV-watching places, which eliminated the arguing over who got to sit where.

Another space issue was where to sit at the dinner table. When their parents are home, they follow a routine, and the seating plan is not an issue. When the parents left, the grandchildren started to argue about where to sit. That was easily settled when I made place cards and gave them assigned seats—*across* the table from each other.

If there is a serious disagreement between or among the children, the best thing to do is to sit down with them and help them work it out. Usually there are two or more sides to the situation. I ask each to tell his side, and if there is no agreement, I have them continue to talk it over until they reach a consensus. If they continue to argue, I withdraw from the conversation until they do reach an agreement (I stay in that immediate area, though). Then I ask them to suggest some other ways to handle the situation that caused the anger.

Basically children are very sensible. They know right from wrong, and they know the family rules. Instead of trying to exert authoritarian control, give them the opportunity to settle their differences through talking. Sometimes one child really is being unfair to the other. Through a calm, open discussion, steps can often be taken to smooth the situation. It's worth a try!

BEWARE THE FOURTH NIGHT!

I first got the idea for this book when I called a good friend while she was babysitting her four grandchildren (all different ages, ranging from first grade to ninth grade) on the fourth night of a ten-day babysitting stint. She was so upset, she was fuming! If anything could go wrong, it had. She is a calm, very organized person who had raised four children of her own and is a retired teacher. But here she was, just as frustrated as I get sometimes when I'm doing extended babysitting.

I realized that I wasn't the only one who was having difficulty at times. And as I talked with other friends, I found that these difficult babysitting situations often occur on the fourth night. It seems that the "honeymoon period" is over by that day. The children are probably missing their parents, and good-natured grandmother is a bit low on energy and is losing her sense of humor. If you realize this ahead of time, you can be more careful to conserve your energy so that you are able to maintain your sense of humor and remain calm. If possible, take a nap that day.

After all, if we want to "Catch the Children Being Good," we must be good to ourselves. It is essential that we get enough rest, remember that things don't have to be perfect, and most important of all, keep our sense of humor. Children will respond to that positive good humor with their own good humor, and everyone will have a good time.

6

FOOD: THE WAY
TO A GRANDCHILD'S HEART

You and your grandchildren can have fun preparing food together while you are babysitting. Before I leave home, I call my grandchildren. Yes, I tell them, they can have pizza and macaroni and cheese—but not every night. What fruits and vegetables (fresh or cooked) would you like? I ask. What special dinners do you want me to fix?

I save recipes that might tempt them, and put them in a three-ring notebook with plastic covers over the pages. My "Grandma's Recipes and Menus" notebook goes back and forth with me every time I visit.

Some day I might even make copies of the book and give them as presents to my grandchildren when they're grown and do their own cooking for their own kids. It would be fun to make notations like: "You could never resist a second helping of this!" or "Remember the first time you tried to make this yourself?"

When I first began to babysit my grandchildren, my daughter, in an effort to be helpful, would do the grocery shopping and put away the groceries before I arrived. We've changed that. First of all, I often had to hunt for a long time to find the exact location of the stored groceries. (It's really aggravating to be in the middle of preparing spaghetti sauce and not be able to locate that elusive fresh garlic, or the canned tomatoes hiding behind the refried beans.) Most importantly though, I wanted to do food projects with the grandchildren, and I wanted them to help with the grocery shopping.

MENU PLANNING

Soon after I arrive, I plan a week's menu with my grandchildren (see sample choices in Chapter 7), and we post it on the refrigerator. But the menu is not written in cement; if, at the last minute, we want to make changes or even go out for dinner, it's perfectly all right. Being relaxed and flexible with the grandchildren about food is a lot of fun.

When I was raising my own children and also teaching, there wasn't much time for flexibility. I used to have a "Week-A Menu" and grocery list, and a "Week-B Menu" and grocery list, and I rotated the weeks. Obviously, I wasn't big on creativity then—there were too many other things needing my attention—so my focus was on serving nourishing, healthful meals in an efficient and timely manner.

FOOD SHOPPING

Now that my grandchildren are old enough to be sensible in a grocery store, I usually take one or both of them along on shopping trips. They are quite helpful with the shopping, and it gives them last-minute choices of food, such as special fruits or vegetables that might be in season. Fresh strawberries, pineapple, blueberries, broccoli, cucumbers, cherry tomatoes, and corn-on-the-cob are favorites. Choosing which dessert they want to fix for dinner is another bonus. (They take turns preparing dessert.) Since the children get to make so many of the food choices, mealtimes go very well.

Before the parents leave, though, I always get a list of "yes" or "absolutely no" breakfast cereals from them. Walking down the cereal aisle in the grocery store with young children is an adventure in itself, and it pays to be prepared.

SNACKS

The key to successful grocery shopping with the grandchildren is to give them a snack *before* going to the grocery store. Entering that veritable wonderland of foods on an empty stomach can be overwhelming, and you wind up with overwrought children. It's not such a bad piece of advice for you, either. Studies have shown that shopping on an empty stomach leads to some very unusual—and fattening—food purchases.

I also find it works well to give my grandchildren a healthful snack before dinner. While preparing the evening meal, I always chop some of their favorite fresh fruits or vegetables (usually vegetables) and put them on a plate on the kitchen counter. It serves as their dinner salad and prevents them from pestering me for cookies or other treats right before dinner.

FOOD ALLERGIES/SENSITIVITIES

When I'm planning meals with the children, I always check with their parents to see if any foods cause negative reactions in them. Food allergies or sensitivities may give certain children headaches or stomachaches, and may also cause them to be hyperactive and/or cranky.

Peanut butter and jelly sandwiches, for instance, have always been a favorite food with both my own children and my grandchildren. They are, after all, the all-American staple food of the growing-up years.

Recently, however, I realized that eating peanut butter triggered headaches in one grandchild. While he was having these headaches, his behavior was overactive, argumentative, and irritable. Now that he is no longer eating peanut butter, my grandchild is back to being his lovable, smiling, and cooperative self. He is also happy not to have those headaches any more.

With his daily peanut butter and jelly sandwich no longer on the menu, my grandson needed help with making other choices for his school lunches. We visited the grocery store together, so he could look at the protein choices and bring some home to sample. Once he understood that peanuts were causing him problems, and that he could make other food choices, he was able to make a successful adjustment to eliminating peanut butter.

During my teaching years I learned to watch for negative physical or emotional behaviors that might be associated with food or drink, such as headaches that may have been caused by wheat or corn products, or stomachaches that may have been caused by dairy products. Chocolate and sugary foods can also cause problems for some children.

If misbehavior is chronic, I have my grandchildren keep a daily food diary. This is a help to them, as it was to my students many years ago. I would say to a student who was having behavior problems that he was a good person, and it was possible that some sort of food or drink might be causing the problem. This approach redirected the focus to the *cause* of the negative behavior. Often a clear pattern emerged, showing a direct relationship between a particular food or drink and the negative behavior.

The parents of my students became rather adept at sorting out food problems for their own children, and they changed the family's food patterns, which quite often helped the whole family. Numerous parents had their children tested by a pediatric allergist to help track down food sensitivities and allergies. Those students showed significant improvement in their academics in school and in their behavior both at school and at home. The children, from third grade on, became aware of which foods to avoid. They were happy to be feeling so much better.

Keep in mind, too, that candy and junk food are not always the culprits—good food can cause problems, too. One of my students was in fifth grade before his very concerned and conscientious mother finally realized that he was allergic to citrus fruits and peanuts. They were some of the "healthy" foods she had been sending to school for his snacks and lunches. Once those foods were eliminated, the improvement in his behavior was dramatic.

If you are concerned about your grandchild's health and behavior, you can be a big help in helping solve the problems. Allergies and sensitivities tend to run in families, and as the person likely to know the most about immediate and extended family members, you might be aware of other relatives who have had specific food problems.

You could keep track of the various kinds of food your grandchild is eating and note the presence of any of the physical problems listed in the checklist on pages 51 and 52. I was the one to suggest that my grandson stop eating peanut-butter sandwiches when I learned that his father is allergic to peanuts.

Of course, some behavior problems have other sources. The use of medication to treat behavior problems in children is a controversial subject, but in the years that I taught children with learning disabilities, some of whom also had attention problems, I learned that there are a few children who need Ritalin or a similar medicine. I saw immediate improvement in those four or five students of mine who began taking it. For many children, however, food and/or environmental allergies/sensitivities are the cause of negative behaviors at school and at home.

A diagnostic approach towards identifying these potential allergies/sensitivities should be taken before progressing to medication. (See the checklists below.) It is essential to identify the cause of the problems instead of trying to just treat the symptoms.

If you want to learn more about this topic, you could begin with books by Dr. Doris Rapp, pediatric allergist (especially *Is This Your Child?*); Dr. William Crook, pediatric allergist (you might find his books in libraries and secondhand book stores); and Dr. Jesse Lynn Hanley, medical director of the Malibu Health Center. The Feingold Association is a significant source of information on allergies, food sensitivities, and allergic behaviors. The association can be found on the Internet at www.feingold.org. If you would like more information on how to follow the Feingold diet, consult Jane Hersey's excellent book, *Why Can't My Child Behave?*

You can find many books that deal with this issue at your library as well as at bookstores and good health-food stores. Also, don't hesitate to trust your own good judgment and experience.

HIDDEN FOOD ALLERGIES/SENSITIVITIES

Hidden food allergies or sensitivities in a child might manifest themselves in the following ways:

Dark circles or "bags" under the eyes _____

Constant sniffling, itchy nose, and clearing of the throat _____

Nervous, irritable, or overactive behavior _____

Tiredness or drowsiness _____

Headaches _____

Stomachaches _____

Frequent respiratory problems _____

Chronic colds and ear infections _____

Digestive problems _____

What health concerns do you have about your grandchild?

_____

_____

_____

POSSIBLE PROBLEM FOOD PRODUCTS

High on the list are products containing:

Wheat _____

Dairy products _____

Corn _____

Sugar _____

Artificial coloring and additives _____

Chocolate _____

Eggs _____

Peanuts _____

Citrus _____

If you suspect your grandchild may have food allergies/sensitivities, note which of the products listed above that the child eats the most. Frequently, the thing a child craves turns out to be the very thing he is allergic/sensitive to. Does the child experience headaches or stomachaches, and/or display negative behaviors after eating any of these products?

_____

_____

COOKING AND BAKING

Children like to cook and bake. My grandchildren particularly enjoy not only deciding what to have for dessert, but also making it. When I'm cooking with them, I use very simple tools that they can learn to use on their own—depending on their ages, of course. For instance, I use a small handheld electric mixer or a mini electric food chopper that is foolproof and easy to use. With the children I never use large food processors or mega do-everything mixers—they're too difficult and too complicated!

I offer "high level" lessons on cooking basics such as how to crack eggs into a bowl—with no shells! A sure-fire method for practicing the technique is to break one egg into a small bowl, check for shells, and if there are none, pour the egg into the larger mixing bowl. The children have learned a lot from reading the directions on boxes of cake, pancake, and cookie mixes and from using measuring cups and spoons to measure various ingredients. The best part of all, though, is eating the delicious dessert they made themselves!

RELAXED DINNERS

As part of our fun approach to meals, my grandchildren and I like to set the mood for the evening dinner. (Breakfast is a relaxed meal only on the weekends, when we cook special food and have the time to eat in a leisurely manner.) But the evening meal can be a pleasant, relaxed time every day.

The lighting is important to us, so we turn off the bright lights in the dining room and use some indirect soft lighting near the ceiling. Usually there is a collection of several candles on the dining table and we light them all. Eating by candlelight is delightful and creates an atmosphere that relaxes adults and children alike. When the parents return and want bright lights with a higher energy level at the table, we talk them into using softer lighting and having a more relaxed time, too.

7

GRANDMA'S RECIPES AND MENUS

Every family has its favorite tried-and-true recipes, some of them time-consuming and others that are of the quick, stir-together, or microwave variety. Now is the time for you to gather some of those child-favorite recipes and put them in your own Grandma's Recipe Book. Your grandchildren will appreciate your thoughtfulness. And don't forget the recipe for your great chocolate-chip cookies.

Here are some of my grandchildren's favorite recipes.

Tuna Melt

A super-simple dish—however, ask your grandchildren exactly how *they* like it made. Recipe makes two sandwiches.

1 (9-ounce) can tuna packed in water, drained

1/8 cup mayonnaise (or the amount you prefer)

4 slices of bread, lightly toasted (be sure it is their favorite brand)

4 ounces shredded cheddar cheese (or their favorite kind of cheese)

Place two pieces of toasted bread on a microwavable plate. Combine the tuna and mayonnaise. Spoon the mixture over the two pieces of toast. Top the mixture with the cheese and heat in the microwave oven for one or two minutes or just until the cheese is melted. Remove from the microwave oven, top with the other slices of toast, cut in half, and serve warm.

Note: This can also be made easily in a toaster oven, using the proper pan. Also, I have learned that there is a "family" way of making even these simple dishes, and if they are prepared differently, sometimes the children won't eat them.

Meatballs

Make a batch of meatballs and freeze them in family-size or individual-size servings. Make them from your choice of meat (ground beef, turkey, chicken, or sweet Italian sausage) and seasonings, depending on what the children like. My Italian Meatballs (see below) taste great simmered in spaghetti sauce (use the children's favorite store-bought brand) and served over pasta, or in meatball sandwiches that are topped with spaghetti sauce and cheese. Often children like them straight-on-a-plate, not mixed with anything. Plain meatballs simmered in leftover or store-bought gravy are good over rice, pasta, mashed potatoes, or straight-on-the-plate.

Tasty Tip: Some children object to onions and garlic in anything, but the cook likes them for the flavor. In that case I use my trusty miniature electric food chopper and totally annihilate any trace of onion or garlic texture, turning them to mush. They are never noticeable in the finished product.

Basic Meatball Recipe

2 pounds lean ground meat

2 eggs, beaten

2 cups bread crumbs, soaked in water or milk, squeezed, and drained

Seasonings of your choice

Combine all ingredients in large bowl and mix with hands. Shape into 1-inch balls. Place meatballs in a baking pan that will catch the drippings. Bake at 350 degrees for 20 to 25 minutes.

Italian Meatballs

To Basic Meatball Recipe add:

$\frac{1}{2}$ pound of Italian sweet sausage

1 tablespoon Italian seasoning

1 tablespoon dried parsley leaves

1 teaspoon salt

1 teaspoon black pepper

$\frac{1}{2}$ cup Parmesan cheese

2 cloves garlic (chopped to mush)

Follow the steps described in the basic recipe.

Plain Beef Meatballs

To Basic Meatball Recipe add:

2 teaspoons basil

2 teaspoons marjoram

2 teaspoons thyme

$\frac{1}{2}$ cup onions (chopped to mush)

Follow the steps described in the basic recipe.

KIS (Keep It Simple) Burgers

When first I planned to cook burgers for the grandchildren, there were many ingredients I wanted to use to make them special. *Wrong!*

They like the plain meat mixed with chopped chives, made into small burgers, pan-fried, topped with cheddar cheese, and served either straight-on-a-plate or on small buns. The small burgers and buns don't overwhelm them, and if they are still hungry they will have a second one. Teenagers, of course, go for maxi-size burgers and buns, with all the other toppings: onions, pickles, tomatoes, lettuce, etc., etc.

Baked Short Ribs

Ribs take slow, low-temperature oven baking, so I make enough to use in a number of different ways, such as in soups, in spaghetti sauce over pasta, in gravy over rice, and in hot beef sandwiches.

4 pounds beef short ribs

1 large sweet onion, chopped fine

1 large clove elephant garlic (or several cloves of regular garlic), chopped fine

1 tablespoon brown sugar

14 ounces broth (I use chicken broth)

2 (28-ounce) cans crushed tomatoes

8 ounces red wine

3 medium pieces Parmesan-Reggiano rinds (optional)

Preheat oven to 275 degrees. Brown short ribs. Remove from pan. Sauté onion and garlic over low heat, about five minutes. Add the brown sugar to the onion and garlic. Stir the liquids and Parmesan rinds into the onion and garlic mixture. Put the ribs back in the mixture and place all the ingredients in a heavy oven pan with a lid. Bake covered for three hours or until tender. Skim fat, shred meat, discard bones, remove rinds, and put meat back in sauce.

Stir-Fried Rice

This is a great recipe for leftovers; it falls into the KIS (keep it simple) category. All the fancy recipes for stir-fried rice are not for those children who want to be able to recognize (and like) every item in the finished product. Since the recipe calls for cooked, cold rice, I always make extra when I'm cooking it for other meals. This is a favorite dinner for the children and is fairly easy to make at the last minute. Add any other favorite leftover vegetables, or fresh bean sprouts if the children like them.

2 tablespoons olive oil

1 small sweet onion, chopped to mush in a miniature electric food grinder

3 to 4 cups of cooked, cold rice

2 cups bite-size pieces of protein (leftover shrimp, beef, ham, poultry, or pork)

Frozen peas, 5 ounces or more

1 or 2 eggs, beaten (quantity depends on how much rice you are using)

Soy sauce (use just a little, depending on the tastes of the family)

It is **essential** that you use a nonstick skillet to prepare this recipe, otherwise you will have a big mess stuck to the pan.

Sauté the onion mush gently in the olive oil for a few minutes in a large, flat, nonstick skillet or a nonstick wok. Once you start adding the other ingredients, keep stirring continuously with a flat-bladed utensil. Add the rice, then the protein, then the peas. When the mixture seems hot throughout, make a well in the center of it, so the bottom of the pan shows. Pour the eggs into it, plus a small amount of soy sauce. Stir the eggs until cooked through, cut into threads with the flat blade utensil and stir them through the rice mixture. Serve hot. This dish can be served as a quick leftover, just by reheating in the microwave oven.

Chinese Food Carryout

There is a terrific Chinese restaurant with carryout food close to the grocery store. When I'm busy and short on cooking time, I buy dinner there. Each child has his or her favorite Chinese dishes, so I keep a list of those choices with me and make a quick stop there from time to time.

Baked Salmon Fillet

This is an easy-to-fix recipe and good for leftovers, so I make about a half-pound for each person, which is more than the children eat. I also prepare a large amount of the sauce, because it is very tasty over rice.

Salmon fillet

Mayonnaise

Mustard

Preheat the oven to 350 degrees. Grease/oil a baking pan or dish with sides. Mix the mayonnaise and mustard to your taste. (Some children don't like a strong mustard taste.) Place the fillet in the baking dish, cover with the mayonnaise/mustard sauce, place in the oven, and bake for about 25 to 30 minutes. Serve with plain cooked rice.

Steamed Shrimp

This is another of the children's favorites. We watch the paper for sales. I've found a seafood shop that has good prices for seniors on Tuesdays, so we tend to eat our seafood dinners around that time of the week. Again, I cook about a half-pound per person, since I use the leftover shrimp for Stir-Fried Rice (see page 58). I cook the shrimp in their shells, and the children peel their own, depending on their age and ability, of course. They like the shrimp plain or dipped in melted butter.

Shrimp in shells

Butter, melted

Bring water to a boil. Then lower the heat; the water should only simmer. Add shrimp and cook covered 3 to 5 minutes (depending on the size of the shrimp). Shells will turn pink/red. Immediately pour shrimp into a colander in the sink, run cold water over the shrimp, and cover them with ice cubes. That stops the cooking so they won't get mushy. Just put them in a big bowl on the table with extra bowls for the shells, lots of napkins, and the melted butter in small individual cups.

Note: I cook the shrimp in two or three batches and just scoop the cooked shrimp out of the hot water each time. I seem to be able to control the water temperature better that way. With the last batch, I dump out all the water with the shrimp.

Pizza

As with the meatballs, I had visions of making extra-special pizzas for my grandchildren. I actually did for a while, but it was labor-intensive. Then I learned that the children had a favorite commercial frozen, self-rising pizza. It even starts in a cold oven. Now that I'm older and wiser, I make sure that one of those pizzas is always in the freezer, ready for a quick, no-fix dinner. I'm careful that I buy the exact brand of their choice, otherwise it just isn't quite right.

Scalloped Potatoes

Needless to say, I buy the children's favorite box mix brand at the store. But, I sometimes cube some ham and add it to the mixture before baking, cooking on top of the stove, or microwaving. Follow the directions on the box.

Macaroni and Cheese

This was a favorite dish of mine when I was growing up. My mother had a special way of making it that would be difficult to replicate. My dad loved hard, aged cheese, which he liked best at room temperature. So there always was a plate of gourmet cheese sitting on the kitchen table where he could sample it as he passed. Needless to say, some of it would get a bit dry, and since my dad didn't want that part, my mother would collect those pieces of cheese and put them in a covered jar in the refrigerator. When she had enough, she would grate it and use it to make macaroni and cheese. It was superb!

Naturally, when I started making this dish for my grandchildren, I tried to make it the way my mother had. I made enough of it to freeze in individual portions for quick meals, but several months later when I came back to visit, those same macaroni and cheese dinners were **still** in the freezer. Just as they had a favorite pizza, the children had a particular macaroni and cheese that they preferred—you guessed it, a commercial brand in a box! I now make sure I have several boxes of their favorite brand of macaroni and cheese in the cupboard.

Pot Stickers

Recently, my grandchildren and I were shopping in an Asian grocery store, and we decided to try something called pot stickers. As it turns out, they are both easy to prepare and delicious. They consist of dough wrapped around various kinds of fillings, usually seasoned vegetables and different kinds of meat, poultry, or seafood. (There are vegetarian versions, too.) Since they come frozen, I buy several kinds (children's choice) to keep at home in the freezer. We use them for a quick lunch or as a dinner side dish. The directions are on the package. Just bring water to a boil, drop in the pot stickers, stir gently so they don't stick to each other, and wait until they float to the surface. Cook for a few minutes more (whatever the directions say) and serve hot.

Roast Chicken

I don't wait for special times to serve this dish, since it is so easy to fix. When you roast the whole chicken each child gets to choose his favorite part, and I use the leftovers for many other dishes. To make the dinner as easy as possible, I use those oven baking bags and fix Stove-Top Stuffing for a side dish.

Baked Chicken and Rice

This is another easy oven-baked dinner that's popular with children. I usually make double the recipe, because the leftovers are great. Just reheat in the microwave oven. If the children don't like mushrooms, just substitute another kind of cream soup for the mushroom soup.

> 1 cup rice, uncooked
> 1 can (10 and 3/4 ounce) cream of celery soup
> 1 can (10 and 3/4 ounce) cream of mushroom soup
> 1 can (10 and 3/4 ounce) cream of chicken soup
> $\frac{1}{2}$ can water
> Chicken pieces (enough to serve four)
> 1/8 cup melted butter

Preheat the oven to 325 degrees. Grease a flat baking dish. Mix the rice, the three soups, and the water in a bowl. When thoroughly blended, pour mixture into the baking dish. Place the chicken pieces over the rice mixture, just one layer high. Pour the melted butter over top of the chicken and cover the pan with foil (or a lid) and bake for two hours. During the last 15 minutes remove the foil (or the lid). Serves four.

Burritos

Good old burritos are a great all-purpose food. They're easy to make and can be eaten hot or cold, vegetarian or with cooked leftover meat or poultry. They can even be brought to school for lunch, packaged in a zip-lock baggie. Each family seems to have its favorite ingredients. This happens to be a KIS (keep it simple) recipe that my grandchildren particularly like. Use flour tortillas, large or small, depending on the ages and appetites of the children. (I tend to use the smaller ones so the burrito doesn't overwhelm the child. Teenagers, of course, will want the large ones.)

> Flour tortillas
> Canned refried beans
> Mild salsa
> Monterey Jack, cheddar or Colby cheese (use the children's favorite), shredded
> Cooked meat or poultry, shredded (optional)

Mix the refried beans and salsa to a soft consistency and heat on the stove. Place a flour tortilla on a microwavable plate. Spoon a mound of the beans and salsa mixture across the middle of the tortilla, top with a layer of meat or poultry (if desired), and then a layer of cheese. Fold the tortilla over the filling and heat in the microwave about 2 minutes or until the cheese is melted.

Cheese Turnovers

This is an even easier version of burritos.

Flour tortillas
Monterey Jack, cheddar, or Colby cheese, shredded

Place a flour tortilla on a microwave plate, put a mound of cheese across the middle of the tortilla, fold the tortilla over the filling, and heat in the microwave oven until the cheese is melted.

Tacos

Tacos are another easy meal that can be prepared with or without meat. Use any combination of the ingredients listed below.

Crisp taco shells (2 or 3 per person)
1 pound of ground beef
Taco seasoning
Canned refried beans, mixed with mild salsa and heated (separate from the meat)
Tomatoes, chopped
Lettuce, shredded
Monterey Jack, cheddar, or Colby cheese, shredded

Fry the ground beef, drain any fat, and add some of the taco seasoning, according to directions on the package. (A word of caution: I've found that using all the taco seasoning in the package can make the tacos too spicy for the children, so I use just some of it to taste.) Place the meat in the taco shells, and top with the refried bean mixture, tomatoes, lettuce, and cheese.

Barbecued Ribs

There are a lot of great recipes for this, some of which I have made. But again, there are some already cooked in the sauce, packed, and just waiting for you in the meat case at the grocery store. My grandchildren like these, so I go with the flow. It's much easier that way.

Bratwurst and Cheese

My favorite way of eating bratwurst is to boil it and eat it in a hotdog bun with sauerkraut. But since my grandchildren don't like sauerkraut, I fix it their way. I boil the bratwurst until warm, cut a lengthwise slice in each, insert a piece of cheese in the slice, heat briefly in the microwave oven to melt the cheese, and place in a bun. Easy! I keep some bratwurst in the freezer for a quick meal.

Lentil Soup

This is easy to make either vegetarian or with meat or poultry. I double the recipe since it is good for leftover meals or quick lunches.

    1 pound ground pork, beef, or turkey
    1 medium sweet onion, crushed to mush in a food chopper
    2 cloves garlic, crushed in with the onion
    2 carrots, chopped bite size
    2 stalks celery, chopped bite size
    1 tablespoon olive oil
    1 teaspoon marjoram
    1 teaspoon dried basil

1 teaspoon cumin

Salt and pepper to taste

6 cups liquid (water, or chicken or vegetable broth)

2 cups uncooked lentils, rinsed

Shredded cheese

Fry the ground pork, beef, or poultry. Remove from the pan, and drain any fat. Sauté the onion, garlic, and celery in the olive oil until the onion is transparent. Add the spices so they blend with the vegetables. Pour in the liquid, bring to a boil, stir in the meat or poultry and lentils, lower the heat, put the lid on the pot and simmer for 45 minutes or until the lentils are tender. After spooning into individual bowls, top with shredded cheese. Serves eight.

When cooking soups for children, remember they tend not to like the special gourmet soups that we adults favor. So keep your homemade soups simple and only add the ingredients that the children like. I enjoy various mushrooms in my special soups. But the children don't.

Add your favorite kid-friendly soup recipe here.

_____

_____

_____

_____

_____

_____

_____

_____

_____

Lentil Burger

This is a tasty vegetarian burger that can be served straight-on-a-plate or in a round bun. Since they freeze well, keep some stashed in the freezer for the grandchild who really doesn't care for beef burgers.

1 pound lentils, simmered 45 minutes, drained

1 carrot, grated

1 medium sweet onion, chopped to mush in a food chopper

2 eggs, beaten

$\frac{1}{2}$ cup bread crumbs

1 teaspoon paprika

1 tablespoon cumin

1 teaspoon chili powder

2 tablespoons barbecue sauce

1 tablespoon olive oil

Preheat the oven to 350 degrees. Sauté carrot and onion in olive oil about 10 minutes. Add to lentils and cool. Combine all ingredients and mix. Make into patties. Bake for 20 minutes on one side, 10 minutes on the other side. Remember to freeze some for future meals.

Protein Waffles

These waffles are an excellent breakfast item! They can't be beat for flavor, they contain protein, and are wheat-free for anyone on a wheat-free diet.

Baking waffles on a waffle iron can be time-consuming, so I make a double batch and freeze them. When you're in a hurry, it is easy to just pop them out of the freezer, heat them in the toaster oven or toaster (with large slots), and eat. This recipe lists the amounts for a double batch. How many waffles does it make? That depends on the size of the waffles you make.

4 eggs, beaten

2 tablespoons vegetable oil

2 cups sour cream

3 cups buttermilk

4 teaspoons baking powder

3 cups oat flour, sifted

1$\frac{1}{2}$ cups soy flour, sifted

1/4 teaspoon salt

Preheat the waffle iron to a light brown setting. Use a basting brush to oil the waffle iron grids (you only need to do this once for each batch of waffles). Use an electric mixer to combine the beaten eggs, oil, sour cream, and buttermilk. Beat until well mixed. Stir the baking powder, oat flour, soy flour, and salt into the liquids. Drop the appropriate amount of waffle mixture on the waffle iron and bake for about 6 or 7 minutes, depending how dark you like your waffles. Eat warm with your favorite topping or let them cool on racks and freeze flat in plastic zip-lock baggies for future use.

Date Muffins

Here is another delicious protein-rich, wheat-free recipe. The muffins freeze well, so I always make a triple batch. I wrap a frozen muffin in a paper towel and reheat in the microwave oven. Once the basic dough is made, I add a lot of extra ingredients, so they tend to get "over-stuffed." Add as many of the extra ingredients as your family likes. This recipe makes 12 large muffins, but you can easily double or triple it.

2 eggs, beaten

1 cup milk

1 tablespoon vegetable oil

2 tablespoons sugar (more if you like them a little sweeter)

$\frac{1}{2}$ cup grated carrots

2 cups soy flour, sifted

1 tablespoon baking powder

1 cup chopped dates

12 ounces blueberries, frozen or fresh

$\frac{1}{2}$ cup sliced almonds (optional)

Preheat the oven to 350 degrees. Use paper muffin cups in the muffin pan or the muffins might fall apart when you remove them from the pan. Use an electric mixer to beat together the beaten eggs, milk, vegetable oil, sugar, and grated carrots. Stir in the soy flour and baking powder until well mixed. Carefully add the dates and blueberries so the blueberries don't get smashed. Divide the mixture into 12 portions and bake for approximately 20 to 30 minutes, until the tops are lightly browned.

You probably have a favorite muffin recipe that you used to make for your children. You might want to list it below.

_____

_____

_____

_____

_____

Your favorite breakfast bread recipe:

_____

_____

_____

_____

_____

Smoothies

Smoothies are drinks made in a blender and can consist of just about whatever you want. The ones I make are for breakfast, so they include my grandchildren's favorite fruit. I usually keep a supply of frozen blueberries and strawberries. If you happen to have fresh fruit, that's even better. I use the tofu that is vacuum-packed and does not have to be refrigerated until it is open. That way I can keep a supply on hand in the cupboard, since it has a long shelf life. Some people use vanilla yogurt instead of the tofu.

I use a strawberry-flavored protein powder from the health-food store, but you should choose your favorite kind and flavor. This recipe makes approximately 4 servings, but the amounts for each ingredient are flexible.

$1\frac{1}{2}$ cups apple juice (more if the mixture is too thick for the blender)

6 ounces of silken soft tofu (the amount is flexible)

1 cup blueberries

1 cup strawberries

1 or 2 scoops of strawberry-flavored protein powder (there is a scoop in the box)

$\frac{1}{2}$ banana (optional, my grandchildren don't like them in smoothies)

$\frac{1}{2}$ cup fresh or crushed canned pineapple (optional)

Place all ingredients in the blender and mix until smooth. My grandson's typical compliment is, "Nana, this is really good. There aren't big lumps in it today." But lumps or not, he likes to have this smoothie every morning that I am visiting.

Cinnamon Butter

I made this treat for my grandchildren several visits ago, and now it is the first thing they ask me to fix. It is extremely easy to assemble; the only trick is that the butter must be at room temperature.

$\frac{1}{2}$ pound butter (room temperature)

$\frac{1}{2}$ pound confectioner's sugar

2 tablespoons cinnamon (more if you like a stronger flavor)

Place all the ingredients in a mixing bowl and beat with an electric mixer until smooth. Store in a covered dish in the refrigerator. The children like it on toast at breakfast and also on toast or crackers as a treat at other times of the day.

Broccoli with Cheese

This is an easy vegetable dish and a favorite with my grandchildren. I chop the tops into bite-size pieces, then I peel the stalks and slice them into the dish, too.

Broccoli (as much as the children like to eat at one meal)
2 or 3 tablespoons of water
Cheddar or Colby cheese (or the kids' favorite), shredded

Place the broccoli and water in a microwavable dish with a lid partly covering it. Microwave for 8 to 10 minutes or until the broccoli is tender. Remove from the microwave oven, drain the water, cover the broccoli with as much cheese as you like. Put back in the microwave for a minute, just until the cheese melts. Serve hot.

List the cooked vegetables that your grandchildren like best. Collect recipes that use those vegetables in a kid-friendly way.

_____

_____

_____

_____

_____

Raw Chopped Vegetables, Straight-on-a-Plate

Even though my grandchildren like fresh vegetables, they each have their individual favorites. In order to give the children a choice, every time I serve raw vegetables—which is almost every night—I simply chop them up and put them out on a plate on the kitchen table, along with their favorite salad dressing in very small bowls (each child likes to have his or her own). They snack away on them while I finish preparing dinner. When the main courses are ready, we sit down together to eat—and they've already had their salad as a snack!

Some of their favorites are:

Lettuce pieces
Cherry tomatoes
Cucumber, peeled and sliced
Summer squash, sliced
Baby carrots
Broccoli
Celery pieces

List the raw vegetables that your grandchildren like best. Serve only those.

_____

_____

WEEKLY MENUS

My grandchildren make the dinner menu choices for the week, and we post them on the refrigerator. They are subject to change, if we decide to trade one thing for another, or if we choose to eat out. The children often check to see what's for dinner, and they look forward to the evening meal.

Since breakfast must be fixed and eaten in an efficient manner on a school day, I have the children decide *for sure* what the breakfast menu will be the next morning. They also decide what they want packed in their lunch for school the next day. We fix as much of the lunch as possible the night before, putting all room-temperature foods into their lunch containers, the ice packs in the freezer, and the juice boxes in the refrigerator. The weekend lunch menu does vary, of course, from the one for school days.

Giving children menu choices, rather than just telling them what to eat, allows them to feel in control of their meals. With this approach, there are no reluctant eaters. It also helps make mealtime a very pleasant time, with a lot of interaction between the children and the adult(s). My grandchildren and I do talk about choosing from the different food groups in order to get balanced meals, but the menu is still their choice. And yes, we can have pizza, and macaroni and cheese—just not every night!

Breakfast Choices

Juice (apple, orange, grapefruit)	Bacon
Smoothie	Ham
	Scrambled eggs and cheese
Muffins	
Oatmeal	
Toast (bread, bagels, English muffins) with cream cheese	Yogurt
Waffles	

Cinnamon butter
Jelly

Add your choices:

_____

_____

_____

Lunch Choices for School

I always make sure that my grandchildren include protein in their lunch boxes. But it can be their choice of leftover meat or poultry, sliced deli meat or poultry, cheese, a cheese burrito, or a bean-and-cheese burrito—just to mention some of the children's favorites. Sometimes my grandson likes his deli meat rolled up and put in a sandwich baggie, to eat without bread, and sometimes he likes to substitute potato chips for the bread. He likes the lettuce in a separate baggie so it stays crisp. He likes his fruit in a separate baggie, too. Who cares how he eats his food? As long as he eats a good balance of foods each day, it is his choice.

Lunch food choices:

Apple

Breakfast bars

Carrots

Celery sticks

Cookies

Grapes

Juice box

Potato or corn chips

Sandwich

Yogurt

Lunch Choices for Home

Choices from the school list:

Bratwurst sandwich

Leftovers from dinner

Lentil soup

Macaroni and cheese

Meatballs

Pizza

Pot stickers

Spaghetti O's

Tuna melt

Your grandchildren's favorite home lunches:

_____

_____

_____

_____

Dinner Choices—Entrées

Bratwurst and cheese sandwich

Burritos

Chicken and rice, baked

Chicken, roasted

Ham

Hamburgers

Lentil soup

Macaroni and cheese

Meatballs

Pizza

Ribs, barbecued

Salmon fillet, baked

Scalloped potatoes with ham

Shrimp, steamed

Short ribs

Spaghetti

Stir-fried rice

Tacos

Tuna melt

Your Grandchildren's Favorite Dinner Choices—Entrées

_____

_____

_____

_____

_____

_____

_____

List some of the dinner entrées that your own children especially liked when they were growing up. Suggest them to your grandchildren. Perhaps they would like to try some of Mommy's or Daddy's childhood favorites.

_____

_____

_____

_____

_____

_____

_____

Dinner Choices—Side Dishes

Broccoli and cheese, steamed

Corn

Green beans

Peas

Plain cooked rice (with soy sauce or butter)

Plain pasta (with butter, cheese, or sauce)

Potatoes (baked, scalloped, or mashed)

Pot stickers

Raw vegetables (tomatoes, lettuce, cucumber, carrots, celery, summer squash)

List your grandchildren's favorite side dishes:

_____

_____

_____

_____

_____

_____

_____

Desserts

I have listed no dessert recipes here, because when my grandchildren and I do the grocery shopping together, they choose what they want to fix for dessert. Instant Jello chocolate pudding happens to be a favorite, as is store-bought angel-food cake with fresh chopped strawberries and whipped cream. We look for easy-to-fix items like slice-and-bake cookies, refrigerated cinnamon rolls in a pop-open tube, and frozen pumpkin pie that goes straight into the oven and bakes for an hour, more or less.

We also spend time in the box-mix section, looking for easy-to-make brownies, cookies, cakes, and such. We stand there and read the directions on the boxes—the simplest ones are often our choice. Of course, ice cream and store-bought cookies are always good when time is short.

As a retired person with time to think about various cooking and baking ideas, I am thoroughly enjoying doing this flexible food approach with the grandchildren. From the time my children were in grade school I was a working mother, and my days were so over-scheduled that I had to be extremely organized with the family meals. Now that I do the extended babysitting for my grandchildren, I have the time to do with these children what I would have enjoyed doing with my own children.

8

TIME FOR FUN

Now for the fun part of being a grandparent! This is what we fantasize about when we think of spending time with the grandchildren. Some of the best times I have when I visit my grandchildren are the special activities that we share.

Prior to my arrival I always ask my grandchildren about their favorite thing to do or their favorite place to go. (They seem to change from one time to the next.) Because there is a significant age span between the children, I plan carefully so each one gets an equal choice of activities. I write to the local chamber of commerce ahead of time, and they send sightseeing information and a list of special events for that season. The children and I also have our favorite restaurants, and we are always sampling new ones.

SEW SPECIAL

In addition to planning to go to favorite or new places, the children quite often choose special costumes they want me to make while I visit. (I like to sew.) They might be for Halloween, special events, or a school play. During my last extended babysitting stint, my grandson had in mind a particular cape that he wanted for his next Halloween costume.

My teenage granddaughter's desire for a Renaissance costume to wear at the summer Renaissance Festival led to a marathon design and sewing project. After hours in a fabric shop, she finally chose the pattern and the fabrics needed for the three separate parts of the costume. Her goal was to design a cotton outfit that would be appropriate for everyday use in a shop in the Renaissance period.

At home we took over the dining-room table for the cutting and sewing, with on-going fittings. Of course, pattern remnants and pins were flying everywhere. Both of us tend to save all the "nice" fabric remnants—although we often have no idea what we're going to do with them—and soon they were piling up. Then my granddaughter had an idea for making a soft pouch out of one of the remnants, which, when finished, was a perfect addition to the costume. Of course that just reinforced our tendency to save the "nice" remnant pieces.

My artistic granddaughter already had a collection of her own paintings (I even have some of them hanging at home), and this designing and sewing project gave her a new medium for expressing her creativity. We have some great photographs of her in the Renaissance costume, standing against a background of summer flowers. This sewing project was definitely the stuff of memories.

HELP WITH HOMEWORK

One of the advantages of extended babysitting is that it gives you time to become deeply involved with your grandchildren and to share in their areas of interest. It is of such shared experiences that we create lasting memories.

Before you embark on a fun project like making a costume with school-age children, however, be sure to check with them to see if they have school projects to finish (or even to *start* and finish). First things first. Working parents often don't have much time to drive to various places for things their children need to get for school projects, and sometimes things get put "on the back burner." (And some children are just natural procrastinators). You can really be a big help at such times.

One time when I was babysitting, my granddaughter had a specific idea in mind for a natural science project. We drove around, made three stops, got what she needed, and she assembled the project in a short time. By starting early, she was able to give the seeds the proper growing time. Since she also needed to do some library research, we did it together and I was able to share some ideas about information collecting and bibliography format.

Note: Be sure you know where the children's library cards are before the parents leave. It is a bother to have to search for the special place in which they are kept.

A TREASURE HUNT

Sometimes we decide to make the extended babysitting period a major book event by going to the public library and checking out 20 to 25 books at a time. One time my grandson was interested in pirates and sunken treasure, so we checked out all the pirate and sunken-treasure books in the library and read through one after another. He also loves to sketch action pictures, so the books prompted him to draw lots of pictures.

During this time he had to write a short booklet for a school assignment. Using what he had learned from all our reading, he drew a sequence of pictures that demonstrated the recovery process used for retrieving treasure from the sunken Spanish ships off the coast of Florida, and wrote a story line beneath each picture.

An additional event evolved from my grandson's reading interest. The following year, my daughter and her husband, their kids, and my husband and I were vacationing on the east coast of Florida. Partly because of my grandson's interest, we had purchased a metal detector and spent time exploring the seashore where the treasure ships he had read about had sunk many years ago. He was very excited to find a metal object encrusted in seashells. When we had it professionally cleaned, a square iron nail was revealed. According to an authority, the piece dates back to the 1700s, a time when there were eleven shipwrecks in that area.

Ready to explore further, we visited two nearby museums. One, the McLarty Museum, was in the immediate area of the eleven shipwrecks. It is on the site where the survivors stayed until they were rescued. Through displays and artifacts, the museum tells the story of the shipwrecks and the experiences of the survivors.

The second museum we visited was the Mel Fisher Museum in Sebastian, Florida. There we saw recovered treasure and interesting artifacts such as an old cannonball, a pottery vase, a fancy goblet, a diamond-and-emerald-studded necklace, and gold and silver coins. A fun activity in this museum is to lift a bar of real gold, one that had been recovered from a sunken treasure ship. This museum was a "must see" for my grandson, since one of his favorite books about recovering sunken treasure was an illustrated children's book about Mel Fisher, who recovered treasure from a ship named *Nuestra Senora de Atocha*.

This whole series of family adventures began with my grandson's interest in pirates and sunken treasure. I was so happy that I had the time to take him to the library and let him explore this interest.

MORE LIBRARY ADVENTURES

Another time my grandson was very interested in snakes. His room was full of books about snakes, drawings of snakes, etc., etc. We went to the library and got more books on snakes and read about them. Then we decided it might be fun to make our own snakes. I bought some solid-color ties for a dollar each at a bargain store, stuffed them, and sewed on some pieces of fabric for eyes and tongues. Of course, we had stuffed snakes draped everywhere.

One summer, all of our book reading helped my grandchildren finish the requirements of the summer reading program at the local public library. Similar programs are offered at most public libraries throughout the United States. They help children improve their reading skills and introduce them to new authors.

Recently, in the public library in Melbourne, Florida, I was talking with the children's librarian about her plans for its upcoming summer reading program. She has titled the program "Start at the Library and Go Anywhere." Each week she has a different speaker, including children's authors, storytellers, a scientist, a naturalist, and someone from the Space Center. About 100 children attend each week. The librarian uses the speakers as a way of drawing children into the library. Volunteers are available after each speech to help the children find books in their areas of interest. The librarian's goal is to help young readers develop interest areas that will lead them to think, learn, and explore.

As I listened to her, I had to smile to myself. My grandchildren and I tend to follow a similar approach to "Start at the Library and Go Anywhere." My grandson's interest in sunken treasure led to those exciting family adventures. My granddaughter's interest in the Laura Ingalls Wilder books about early settlers in the Midwest led us on a daylong trip to the original Wisconsin homes of two of her favorite authors. These historical sites provided us with a lot of additional information on the pioneers. Plus, it was a fun day!

The very best way to get children interested in books is to visit the children's section of the public library. (Wear comfortable clothes, since you will be sitting on the floor with the children while you all are hunting through books.) If the children already have a particular interest, I always ask the librarian for assistance in finding all the books on that subject. Otherwise, let your grandchildren look on their own for subjects that catch their fancy. Children are naturally curious and will be drawn to books in their own areas of interest.

My favorite type of children's books are natural science stories about real animals, plants, fish, and birds and other scientific subjects that have been written at a primary reading level. They can be used to read aloud to preschool children, and are excellent for children who are learning to read. Kids especially like these types of books because they enjoy learning "real" information. Books like these have a high content level, but are written to be read and understood by beginning readers. The child's reaction often is, "Wow, did you know that . . . ?" Books are truly a window to the world!

Since we tend to check out books in volume, I always get a printout from the librarian that lists the entire lot, and I have canvas carrying bags that I use to keep the books somewhat contained at home. Before I leave my grandchildren to come home, I always return all of the books to the library. That computer printout of all the books we checked out comes in very handy. We can go down the list and be sure every book is returned on time.

ANOTHER TREASURE HUNT

My grandchildren's and my interest in museums, rocks, outdoor activities, and exploring once led to a most intriguing series of events. One summer day, while we were examining some fossils in a rock shop, the shop owner told us about Lily Dale Park, across the river from St. Paul, Minnesota, where there is an excellent location for digging fossils. In order to dig there we had to have written permission from the Lily Dale Park Service.

Note: It is important to remember that you can only dig and collect fossils in designated areas. In many places (national parks, for example) it is against the law to remove artifacts. Be aware of rules and laws in your area.

A few days later, after we had gotten ourselves organized with backpacks, plastic storage containers, picnic lunches, and water bottles, the children and their friends and I set off for the dig. The night before there had been a raging downpour, leaving the hiking trail and dig site a massive, muddy mess. When we reached the designated dig site, however, we realized that the rainstorm had moved a significant amount of soil, leaving the fossils exposed to the sunlight. We sat there and picked and collected for quite a while, sharing various finds with each other. Finally we decided that we had enough fossils, and it was way past lunchtime. The only problem was that all of us were coated with mud. No matter how hungry we were, we would have to shed the mud somehow. While walking back down the path, winding our way through a heavy growth of trees and shrubs, we discovered a lovely, twisting brook. It was, however, surrounded by steep banks, making it somewhat inaccessible to us.

By that time the temperature had risen to such an extent that we were all very hot—as well as mud-caked—so we were highly motivated to get in the stream to play, clean up, and get cool.

We followed the stream until all of a sudden I realized I couldn't see my grandson. Then I heard him splashing and laughing. Not only had he discovered a small path down to the stream, but he was playing in a waist-deep pool, located partly under a small waterfall. Needless to say, we all shed our shoes and went splashing, fully clothed, into the stream and the pool.

Sunbeams at times pierced through the overhanging trees, spotlighting the moss and small flowers nestled in among the rocks. This miniature world was cool, shaded, and somehow very special. At last, refreshed and considerably less muddy, we settled down on some flat rocks, located midstream, and ate a leisurely lunch. Fortunately, I had my camera along that day, and I have keepsake photos to remind us of a wonderful experience. The time we spend with our grandchildren can put us in the play mode—and give us so many cherished memories.

The next day, while examining our "treasures," we realized we could not identify any of the pieces. So we set off on another adventure— St. Paul's Science Museum, where we spent our time hunting for identical fossils. We learned our fossils were from an ancient period of time when that part of the Midwest was under an ocean. Interestingly enough, all the fossils we found were either a form of shellfish or aquatic plant.

FINDING FUN

Even mending can take a turn toward fun and games. One time when I was trying to mend my grandson's jeans—torn through at the knees, of course—I realized that the best thing to do was cut them off at the knees and make them into shorts. When my grandson saw the cut-off bottom pieces, he decided that they would make perfect treasure bags for him. Well, that certainly was an easy project for Nana—seam up the bottom and put a drawstring at the top. He was delighted, and he still uses those "treasure bags."

What are *your* special talents, interests, and hobbies? Share them with your grandchildren! The range of special activities you can enjoy together is as wide as your imagination.

Listed below are some books that discuss interesting activities for grandparents to do for and with their grandchildren.

Grand Activities, by Shari Sasser, Career Press, 1999. Excellent fun activities.

The Grandmother Principles, by Suzette Haden Elgin, Abbeville Press, 2000. Crafts, family history projects, and more.

How To Be A Way Cool Grandfather, by Verne Steen, Mustang Publishing Co., 1996. A great book for projects, with clear, simple directions.

Long-Distance Grandma, by Janet Colsher Teitsort, Baker Books, 1998. Month-by-month activities to help you keep in touch; the grandparent organizes the activities and send them to the grandchildren.

The Nanas and the Papas, by Kathryn and Allan Zullo, Andrews McMeel Publishing, 1998. Appendix has Web sites, newsletters, organizations, grandchild safety tips, and information on grandparent-grandchild travel.

FAVORITE PLACES TO GO

_____

_____

_____

_____

_____

_____

FAVORITE THINGS TO DO

_____

_____

_____

_____
_____
_____
_____

FAVORITE RESTAURANTS

_____
_____
_____

SPECIAL PROJECTS TO DO

_____
_____
_____
_____
_____
_____

SPECIAL BOOKS TO READ

_____
_____
_____
_____
_____
_____

9

ONCE UPON A TIME

Sharing family history with our grandchildren is one of the most valuable gifts that a grandparent can give. The big question is how best to do it. There are numerous books and programs on the market that explain how to create family trees, send e-mail photos, and organize any information that a person has. All of these things take time and some also require a fair knowledge of the computer world.

On the other hand, an interesting thing happened to me while I was researching and writing this chapter. I discovered how very helpful local libraries are. There are enthusiastic, informative volunteers to help you start your search for your roots, classes that will teach you how to use the computer in your search, various monthly magazines, monthly meetings, computer software that specializes in genealogy, and information about genealogical societies. The local library may also have printed forms that you can use to record family-tree information as you go.

Since many children today have extensive computer experience, a genealogical search would be a fun project to do with them. If I can become more confident about my ability to use computers to do research, there is hope for all.

SEARCHING FOR YOUR ROOTS ON THE WEB

To facilitate your computer genealogical research with your grand-children, I've compiled a list of Web sites that you can explore to-gether.

Cyndi's List   http://www.cyndislist.com
Cyndi's List is undoubtedly the most extensive genealogical site on the Internet. They have more than 90,200 links, and almost 20 million people have used the site for online research since 1996. Whatever piece of genealogical history you are looking for, Cyndi's List can point you in the right direction.

LDS Family History Center   http://www.familysearch.org
This site is run by the Mormon Church and has been gathering information on ancestors most of the years it has been in existence.

Roots Web   http://www.rootsweb.com
Roots Web is a directory of free genealogical tools that will help beginners and experienced genealogists alike. It is one of the oldest and best in the online genealogy game. There are step-by-step research guides and a reference desk, and if you hit a roadblock, you can even link to Ask-a-Genealogist. It is a site host for many databases containing more than 54 million names.

Genealogy Spot   http://www.genealogyspot.com/
Genealogy Spot is one of the easiest sites of this type to navigate. It has links to just about anything to do with genealogy, but the best thing about the site is that it directly links to nine sites for kids.

Two of the best kid sites are:

Genealogy Today Jr.   http://www.genealogytoday.com/junior
Designated a "family-friendly site," it is full of news, research info, activities, and safe-surfing tips. Kids can even ask the resident expert, Ms. Judy, questions about genealogy research.

My History   http://www.myhistory.org/kids
The activities on this site include making your own family tree, learning how to interview parents and grandparents about their experiences, and saving such family treasures as photographs, letters, and memorabilia. The "How to Do an Interview" page is outstanding. They even provide sample questions and explain what oral histories are. As they point out, your family isn't getting any younger.

USGenWeb Project   http://www.usgenweb.com/researchers/researcher.html
The USGenWeb Project has been described as the premier destination for all genealogists researching American ancestors. It depends on volunteers to maintain the records. Its best feature is the "Help for Researchers" pages, where you can learn such things as the most common mistakes made in genealogy research, seventeen ways to find a maiden name, and how to write and use queries in your research.

There's also a kids' site called:

USGenWeb Kidz   http://www.rootsweb.com/~usgwkidz
This site has a kids' forum, a Webmaster who answers questions, and a section called "How To Do Genealogy."

Genealogy.Com   http://genealogy.com/press
This site has many articles on topics relating to genealogy.

As you begin to explore your genealogy with your grandchildren, you may discover many interesting things about your ancestors. Better still, you'll learn more about your family's youngest generation—your grandchildren themselves. Happy exploring.

TELL US ABOUT THE TIME . . .

There are, however, many stories that will never be found in any genealogical search—your family stories! What did Mom/Dad do at my age or as a baby? Only you know. Just as in bygone years, when older people shared their favorite stories with the children, you can share your memories with your grandchildren. These stories don't always start with "Once upon a time. . . ." Sometimes the stories start other ways.

Remember the "icing on the cake"—the end-of-the-day back rubs, songs, and stories? Well, one such time led to a wonderful family story-telling experience for me. It finally was lights-out time for my young grandson. We were talking about Grandpa's arrival the next day and how many fun things we were going to do. There was a pause in the conversation and then my grandson asked me, "Grandma, how did Grandpa get you to like him?" Was I going to pass up the opportunity to share this information with him? Of course not!

The next day, shortly after Grandpa's arrival, our grandson repeated the entire story that I had told him the night before. Both Grandpa and I were very touched by our grandson's interest in our early friendship.

When we are with our grandchildren for any sustained length of time, many opportunities like this arise. Sometimes it is food or a picture or clothing that will trigger a story about Mom or Dad. The grandchildren always seem eager to hear what their parents were like when they were young.

When you tell stories about your childhood, you also teach your grandchildren. They not only learn a lot about you, but about history. (Face it, at your age you *are* part of history.) The anecdotes you tell about your ancestors—Aunt Mary or Uncle Tom or Great-grandmother Sarah—make the grandchildren more aware of their heritage and family history.

Telling stories is always a lot of fun. Little kids and big kids alike love to listen to them. The more you tell, the more they want to hear. One day a friend of mine was telling stories to her three-year-old grand-daughter. The child looked at her in amazement when she switched from a family story to the story of the "Three Little Pigs," hoping this would lull the child to sleep. "Grandma," she exclaimed, "do you have a book in your head?"

She had been read to by her parents, but they never just told a story and she thought it was just fantastic that people could have stories "in their heads."

If you have family videos, bring some along to share with your grandchildren. And you might even consider taking along the baby book filled with information about and pictures of their Mom or Dad.

This is also a good time to take your old family photos and organize them, placing them in individual albums with the grandchildren. Let them label all the pictures with names, dates, places, and tell them the story that goes with each one.

Don't make family history complicated—just share it!

10

EMERGENCIES: SOS

If you're going to be babysitting for any length of time, you will be serving as the acting parent, and you must have all the essential information, especially in case of an emergency or a health problem. The more prepared you are, the more comfortable you will be.

LETTER OF PERMISSION

The first essential item that you need is a "letter of permission," which says that you have full responsibility for the children for a specific length of time. Here is a format you might use:

(Your name) _____ has full responsibility for my children, (give names) _____, _____, _____, _____, from (starting date) _____ until (ending date) _____. This includes seeking medical and dental care and dealing with all school-related issues.

Parent(s) name(s) _____

Signatures _____

Date _____

PARENTS' ITINERARY

In addition to the letter of permission, you'll need the complete itinerary of the parents. You need to know where they will be the entire time.

Parent contact information:

Hotel name _____

Hotel address _____

Hotel phone number _____

Parent's pager number _____

Parent's cell phone number _____

Date of departure _____

Date of return _____

Airline _____

Flight number and departure time _____

Flight number and return time _____

Who is responsible for parents' transportation to and from the airport? _____

HEALTH CARE DOCUMENTS

Now that you have the letter of permission (*signed* by the parents) and the parents' itinerary, put them in a safe place. In that same place, put information and identification cards that are related to the grandchildren's medical care.

As soon as possible, locate the following items for each child and put them with the letter of permission:

Health Insurance/HMO identity card _____

Rx card _____

Medical ID card _____

Clinic card _____

Military dependent ID card _____

Other identity cards _____

_____

_____

HOME HEALTH CARE

You're just falling asleep and you hear one of the children coughing or sneezing. When you feel the child's forehead, you realize that he has a mild temperature. Obviously this is not an emergency. That means, of course, that you must now play a new role—Dr. Grandma. It's up to you to figure out what to do, and calling the parents in the middle of the night isn't the answer. Again, before the parents leave, have them give you all the information pertaining to the children's medications.

Medication information that you need:

Age and weight of each child (dosage is often determined by weight) _____

Prescription medicines and locations _____

Who gets which prescription medicine? _____

When is the prescription medicine given? _____

What over-the-counter medicine for headache? _____

What over-the-counter medicine for temperature? _____

What over-the-counter medicine for tummyache? _____

What over-the-counter medicine for cough? _____

Who is allergic to what medicine? _____

Who is allergic to what foods or other substances? _____

Where is the small humidifier kept? _____

Where are the cough drops kept? _____

Where are the thermometer and first aid kit kept? _____

Do any of the children have any chronic or recurring illnesses (asthma, croup, ear infections)? _____

How should these be treated? _____

_____

_____

_____

PROFESSIONAL HEALTH CARE

Hopefully you will never have to use the following names and phone numbers except for routine appointments. If, however, you do need emergency health or dental care for the children, the information is ready for you. Remember: You will need to take the letter of permission to the professional caregiver before medical attention can be given to the child. Emergency care can be administered, of course, but you need that letter. It is also imperative that you call the parents as soon as possible, which means having the parents' itinerary immediately available.

Essential information:

Doctor _____

Doctor's phone _____

Doctor's address _____

Directions _____

_____

Hospital name _____

Hospital phone _____

Hospital address _____

Directions _____

_____

Pharmacy _____

Pharmacy phone _____

Pharmacy address _____

Directions _____

_____

Poison control center _____

Poison control center phone _____

Emergency-911

Fire department phone _____

Police department phone _____

Dentist _____

Dentist's phone _____

Dentist's address _____

Directions _____

Additional medical emergency information _____

PET EMERGENCIES

If there are pets in your care, you will also need a second letter of permission that says that you have full responsibility for the pet(s) for a specific length of time.

Letter of Permission for Pets

Below is a format you might use:

(Your name) _____ has full responsibility for my dog(s) or cat(s), (give names) _____, _____, _____,
from (starting date) _____ until (ending date) _____.
This includes seeking emergency medical care. I do want to be informed immediately, however, so that I may decide the length and depth of medical care that is appropriate and the costs that might be incurred.

Pet owner's name _____

Date signed _____

Emergency Information for Pets

Veterinarian _____

Veterinarian's phone _____

Veterinarian's address _____

Directions _____

_____

_____

Does the pet have any health problems? _____

_____

Other information: _____

_____

SCHOOL EMERGENCIES

Teachers at the elementary level need to know that you are going to be in charge of the children for a given length of time. The parents can either introduce you in person when dropping off the children at school, or they can send a note. This is essential if you need to pick up your grandchildren at school for a special activity or a medical appointment. A school administrator might want to see that signed permission letter, too.

While I'm meeting the elementary teachers, I like to volunteer to help chaperone field trips or to help in the classroom. The teachers quite often take me up on my offer—and my young grandson is always glad that I'm there.

When you think about school emergencies, you tend to think in terms of medical emergencies that might have happened at school. Keep in mind, however, that other kinds of emergencies could arise. For example, the school principal might call to say there is a problem with your grandchild, and you, as the substitute parent, must come in and discuss the situation.

Should this type of problem present itself, first take a deep breath and calm yourself. Before going to the school, take the time to put on some nice clothes, fix your makeup, and comb your hair. (Grandfathers, you can skip the makeup.) When you are talking with the principal, stay calm and sensible. The problem needs to be discussed by you and the principal alone first, and then with the child present. It is essential that the child understands exactly what he did wrong. Most likely the child will need to go home right then, and you will need to think of a responsible, sensible punishment for him.

One approach that seems appropriate for elementary children is a time-out in the child's bedroom for the rest of the day. The child may only leave the bedroom for dinner and to go to the bathroom. No one may talk or interact with the child during that time. At dinnertime the child can sit at a separate table. By bedtime you should be present to tuck the child in bed and to talk gently with him about comforting things. This day is over, and tomorrow is another day. The next morning before school, interact in a pleasant way with the child and send him off to school with a hug and a kiss.

An appropriate punishment for an older child might be the loss of phone privileges for a day or so. Or no TV. Or no computer games/e-mail. You walk a fine line here. The child needs to be held accountable for the serious misbehavior at school. (If it were not serious, the principal would not have called.) At the same time, it is not the end of the world.

As a former school administrator and teacher, I know that students sometimes exhibit negative changes in behavior while their parents are away. Sometimes it happens when only the mother is away, because the father left in charge at home isn't used to the daily responsibilities, and life gets out of kilter at times. Again, it isn't the end of the world. Life just needed to be smoothed over a bit.

School Directory

School information that you need for each child:

Child _____

School name _____ phone _____

School address _____

Teacher's name _____

Child _____

School name _____ phone _____

School address _____

Teacher's name _____

Child _____

School name _____ phone _____

School address _____

Teacher's name _____

Directions to schools:

_____

_____

_____

_____

AFTER-SCHOOL PROGRAMS

If the children go to an after-school child-care program, the supervising adults there must be notified that you will be babysitting. They should also get a copy of the letter of permission. Since you will be picking up your grandchildren from the program, the caregivers must know who you are. In some cases you may be asked to show identification. Of course, the fact that the grandchildren run up to you shouting, "Grandma! Grandma!" might be all the identification you need! However, it's good to know the policies ahead of time.

The biggest mistake you can make with daycare centers is to show up after the pickup deadline. You will be charged big bucks by the minute and will be facing some very unhappy caregivers. I have had two close calls: one when I got lost in major traffic and took the wrong exit, and the other time when there was a surprise 27-inch snowfall in March. (In Minnesota, what can you expect?) I can live without that kind of anxiety, so I start early, avoid big traffic areas, and at the first snowflake I am on my way to the child-care center.

After-school information that you need to know:

Daycare center name _____ phone _____

Daycare center address _____

End-of-day pickup time _____

Directions _____

_____

NEIGHBORS

When I first started babysitting for extended periods, I often wondered which neighbor would be a good person to call in an emergency. I knew that some neighbors could be your best help—or your biggest problem. I'd just as soon avoid the ones who don't like hearing the family dog bark, or the ones who want my grandchildren to stay away from their yard full of flowers.

I could always have asked the grandchildren about the neighbors, but I felt it was best to talk with my daughter and son-in-law about who might be the most helpful neighbor should I ever be in need of assistance. It's a good idea to be introduced to that neighbor before the parents leave.

Important "helpful neighbor" information:

Name _____

Phone _____

Address _____

Other information _____

Name _____

Phone _____

Address _____

Other information _____

COMMUNITY CONTACTS

Your grandchildren may interact with different members of the community, including parents of school playmates, parents of other children in a weekly shared playtime or activity, recreation center leaders, coaches, or scout leaders.

When I first began to babysit, these names would go right over my head, and there were missed meetings because I didn't know who to call for specific information.

Now is the time to make a list of these names:

Sports coach _____ phone _____
Practice athletic field address/directions _____
_____

Scout leader _____ phone _____
Meeting place address/directions _____
_____

Parents of friends _____ phone _____
Meeting place address/directions _____
_____

Parents of friends _____ phone _____
Meeting place address/directions _____
_____

Additional community person _____ phone _____
Additional community person _____ phone _____

ARE YOU PREPARED?

Of course you are. It can be disconcerting to see all of this absolutely important information that needs to be recorded. But think what would happen if you were babysitting, and any one of the emergencies occurred, and you *weren't* prepared. Just remember, the more prepared you are, the more comfortable you will be.

By this time you must be very comfortable!

11

WHAT DO YOU MEAN I'M *HOUSE*-SITTING?

When you are babysitting grandchildren, you tend to think in terms of just the children. Actually, though, you are also house-sitting. And sometimes the house problems are the ones that really put your teeth on edge. On the following pages are some household horror stories that actually happened to me while I was babysitting.

I KNOW WHERE THE KEY IS!

Peace and quiet at last! I can remember the first year that my own two children were both in school for the first time. The house was quiet, I could think complete thoughts, and at last I could get the whole house somewhat organized.

Well now the "Big Kids" were finally out of the house and on a plane for their business trip. It had been a last-minute hassle as they prepared to leave their place of business well-organized and, hopefully, in safe hands. They had thrown their business clothes into suitcases, hugged and kissed the "Little Kids" (and me, too), and rushed out to the waiting taxi.

The next day, the "Little Kids" were safely off to school and, as before, the house was quiet. I could think complete thoughts and at last get the place somewhat organized again. But, as a friend said after she had been babysitting twin granddaughters, "We be old." Well, perhaps not *that* old, but certainly older than when we were raising our own children. So, instead of organizing the house, I decided to take a leisurely stroll down the street and enjoy the fresh air. In the few days I had been in Minneapolis there had been 23 inches of snow, a deluge of driving rain, a seemingly endless amount of mud, and today the sunshine had finally broken through. Possibly there was an end to this "endless" winter. After all, it was the middle of March.

As I was meandering along, I noticed some large signs nailed and tied to posts and trees. They said: NO PARKING DURING THIS 24-HOUR TIME PERIOD. Not knowing what that was all about, I continued on my way to the small neighborhood store on the next corner to buy some milk and eggs. When I asked the store owner about the street notices, he said they had been posted yesterday, and today was the annual street cleaning. He said the city was very strict about having all vehicles removed, and if I had a car parked out there, I had better move it immediately or it would be towed.

As I rushed out of the store, I could see a tow truck backing up to my son-in-law's 20-year-old, huge, flatbed lumber truck—a truck that was so ornery and eccentric that only my daughter and son-in-law were able to get it to do what it was designed to do. Even though it had been parked right in front of the house, never in my worst nightmare had I ever planned to drive it.

But the thought of paying all that money for the towing ticket, plus paying for all the days that it would be impounded until my daughter and son-in-law could return and retrieve it—well, that certainly pushed my panic button.

The tow truck driver, with hook and chain in hand, was approaching the front of the lumber truck when I raced in front of him. With my back to the truck and my arms outstretched, I started pleading with him not to tow the truck. But it wasn't until I was face-to-face with him that I realized with a jolt that perhaps I shouldn't have been so impulsive.

This burly, blonde-haired giant, taken completely by surprise, stopped—but only briefly. Breathing heavily, nostrils flared, eyes almost squinted shut with anger, he tried to push his way past me, all the time yelling at me to get out of the way. No matter how much I pleaded with him about not towing the truck, he was unmoved.

Finally, in total frustration, I started to cry. Well, he relented somewhat, shouting that he would give me five minutes to move the truck. More tears—I didn't know how to drive the monstrosity, *but* I knew where the key was kept. Gruff, but kind person that he was, the man barked at me to get the key immediately, and he would move the truck off the street.

I'm not sure what the top speed was for that old lumber truck, but he "top speeded" it in reverse to a safe parking space next to my son-in-law's garage. So much for peace and quiet in my life!

I thanked the man several times. Over the years I have remembered him for helping me out of a very difficult and potentially expensive situation.

The moral of this story is: When you are babysitting, know the location of *all* household-related keys. Have your daughter/son make a list of them and where they're located, or make a copy of the list that follows for her/him to complete. (There is also a list in the Appendices at the back of this book.)

Locations of keys for:

House _____

Car _____

All other vehicles _____

Storage areas _____

Garage _____

Bike locks _____

Other _____

_____

Special instructions regarding locks _____

_____

Information on car or house alarm systems _____

_____

PARKING

Be sure to ask your daughter/son about such seemingly unimportant things as parking. Are there any special parking rules you need to know about? Some towns have resident-only parking rules—you may need a visitor's parking permit for your car. Also find out about parking restrictions based on time: some towns don't allow overnight parking on the street. And, in the confusion of the parents' departure, be sure another car doesn't block in the car that you are going to be driving.

DOES ANYONE KNOW A GOOD PLUMBER?

Let's see now, the dinner was good fun, with the school talk and shared experiences. The dishes were in the dishwasher, and the children were getting ready for bed. "Well, it was another busy day, but as soon as stories are read and lights are out, I will be able to catch my breath," I thought.

Then a voice from upstairs called, "Grandma, the tub won't drain!"

Those were not exactly the words I wanted to hear. "Just pull the plug and it will drain," I replied.

"I did that and nothing happened."

The tub was, as usual, filled up as high as it would go, just below the overflow outlet. The depth of water made for great boat sailing or floating or imagining you are at an indoor Disney Water Park. I wondered, do Disney's Water Park specialists make house calls to undo stopped-up tubs? Most likely not. Well, perhaps the tub would slowly drain during storytime.

Later, after the kiddies were tucked into bed—with one last drink of water each—I took a closer look at the water level in the tub. Not even an inch lower! I checked to see that all the toys and washcloths were out of the tub, and I couldn't see anything obvious that would be blocking the flow of water. I looked around for some container to use to start bailing. Well, perhaps it would slowly drain overnight. That seemed like a good plan at the time. I'd think about it tomorrow.

First thing the next morning, however, I heard, "Grandma, the tub still didn't drain."

Sure enough, the water had not gone down even one inch, and using a plunger didn't budge the blockage at all. Obviously, it was time to call in a plumber, but which one?

Here I was, 1,200 miles from home in a strange city, and I needed a plumber. Even when I'm at home, I don't always know which plumber I can get on short notice. And this house, which is almost 100 years old, always seemed to need some sort of "fix-it" person. I was just lucky that it was a stopped-up tub, not a burst pipe. I didn't even know where to turn off the main water connection, if that had been necessary.

The moral of this story is: When you babysit for any period of time, make sure you have the name and number of a good plumber.

DOES ANYONE KNOW ANYTHING ABOUT FURNACES?

During another babysitting trip to Minnesota, a cold front blew through the area, causing the temperature to drop 30 degrees. Of course I immediately turned up the thermostat but—nothing! No heat. I suspected the pilot light on the furnace was out. But all I knew about the furnace was that it was somewhere in the basement.

Would I need another "fix-it" person, or was just a simple adjustment to the furnace required? I called my daughter, and fortunately she was able to tell me what to do, a simple adjustment. If it were something more serious, though, I would have had to call some heating business for assistance. Obviously there was a lot about the house that I needed to know.

The moral of this story is: You'll also need the names and numbers of an electrician and a heating company.

Information you should have (and hopefully won't need):

Plumber _____

Plumber's phone _____

Electrician _____

Electrician's phone _____

Heating/furnace company _____

Heating company's phone _____

Appliance repair shop _____

List the locations of the:

Thermostat(s) _____

Fuse boxes _____

Main water connection _____

Water meter _____

Alarm system (codes, passwords, how to operate it) _____

Flashlights (that work) and extra batteries _____

Basic tools (including a variety of screwdrivers) _____

That very important plunger for the toilet _____

Lightbulbs _____

Candles and matches—in case the lights go out _____

Other house quirks you should know about (such as any plugs or appliances that you shouldn't use because they'll blow the circuits): _____

It would be very helpful to know the location of the instructions for operating the myriad of appliances in the house, including:

TV/VCR _____

CD/tape player _____

Microwave _____

Garbage disposal _____

Washer _____

Dryer _____

Other _____

You might also ask for the location of the nearby video rental store and get the rental card.

THE GARBAGE MAN COMETH, THE GARBAGE MAN LEAVETH

When I'm babysitting grandchildren, I do a lot of cooking—the kind of soups and casseroles that can be frozen for future use for the family. And since I only seem to be able to prepare food in "army-cook" quantities, I accumulate significant amounts of garbage, as well as trash for recycling.

"Well," I thought on a recent trip in March, "that garbage thing is under control, because the collection days and hours are now marked on the calendar." During a previous trip I hadn't known the collection time, and one day I chased after the garbage truck with a parka thrown on over my flannel nightgown. No problem this trip!

This time I had put the garbage in the outside can the evening before, and then put the can out on the street. It had started snowing that evening, and I didn't want to have to deal with the can early in the morning. No, this time I wanted to be prepared. No more chasing the garbage truck at 6 A.M. It's really exasperating to miss the garbage collection and be left with a disgusting, overflowing can.

Early the next morning, while I was fixing French toast for breakfast, I looked out the window and watched incredulously as the garbage truck bypassed my overloaded garbage can. Oh no! This couldn't be happening again.

I did the parka-and-snow-boots routine and chased the garbage truck, calling to the men to take my garbage. They yelled back that they didn't empty cans that were blocked by snow. Sure enough, a snowplow had come through during the night, adding another foot to the two feet of snow that had already accumulated around the can.

I grabbed the first thing I could find—an ineffective old broom—and pushed against the snow in front of the can. It didn't help. Finally, in desperation, I grabbed the can and yanked as hard as possible, trying to jerk it over the heap of snow deposited by the snowplow and into the street. It didn't budge!

The garbage men saw me and must have taken pity, because they backed up the truck and said, "That's okay, lady. We'll take your garbage." (I suppose they didn't want me to have a heart attack right there in the street!) Here were more seemingly gruff men who took the time to stop and help a person in need.

The moral of this story is: Sometimes you just don't have all the information you need. You know what happens to people who think they've got everything under control!

Garbage collection information:

Day(s) _____

Time _____

Recycling _____

Other information _____

_____

SNOW SHOVELS, BROOMS, SEASONAL EQUIPMENT

That same snowfall caused another problem. In my daughter's city, residents must clean the snow and ice off public sidewalks in front of their houses within 24 hours. Now I needed a snow shovel. But the last time the grandchildren had seen it was when they were building a snow fort in February. Besides, who would think you'd need a snow shovel in the middle of March?

List the locations of:

Snow shovel _____

Good broom _____

Scraper for ice/snow on the car _____

WHERE IN THE WORLD AM I? OR WHO'S GOT A MAP?

One day I was driving a carload of perishable groceries (which I had wanted to get in the refrigerator before picking up the grandchildren from an athletic field) and suddenly realized that I was lost!

It dawned on me that I had been traveling east for twenty blocks on 25th *Avenue*—when I should have been traveling on 25th *Street*. By then

I wasn't even sure which way to drive to correct this mistake. South? West? Or . . . ? Oh, who knew by this time! I was thoroughly lost. I pulled over to look at the city map, but it was difficult to read the very fine print through my tears of frustration.

Here I was, driving around looking for the athletic field where the soccer team was practicing, knowing that practice would be over in five minutes, and just knowing I would never find the field in that short time. I was overwhelmed with frustration! In my mind's eye I could envision a carload of tired, hungry youngsters waiting for me . . . and waiting for me. I finally got there, but only after many anxious moments.

On the way home, after dropping off my grandchildren's teammates, I drove right by my daughter's house. It was pretty embarrassing to have my four-year-old grandson ask if we were going home—and if so, why had I just driven past the house?

There are two morals to this story: First of all, don't participate in car pools when babysitting in a city, where it is so easy to get lost. Your daughter or son can arrange to have other parents do the driving while you're babysitting.

Second, buy a detailed street map, make an enlarged copy of the area, and have it laminated. I use colored pens to mark all pertinent locations on this "permanent map," and I keep it in a special drawer at home where it is always ready to go when I babysit the grandchildren.

Street locations to mark on your map:

House _____

Schools _____

Playgrounds _____

Athletic fields _____

Grocery stores _____

Hospital _____

Doctor _____

Dentist _____

Veterinarian _____

Pharmacy _____

TO WATER OR NOT TO WATER?
THAT IS A GOOD QUESTION!

I am a plant lover, and greenery fills my home and office. For this reason, I'm sure that my daughter felt that I would take excellent care of her plants during her absence. In fact, by the time she returned from one business trip, several of her plants had taken a significant turn for the worse, some even turning a strange shade of yellow. Her lovely collection of orchid plants, which she tends with great care, were the ones in the worst shape.

To water or not to water? That was the question I had asked myself each day. Most of her indoor and outdoor plants needed watering, but I wasn't sure which or how much.

The moral of this story is: You should get some information about the plants you'll be taking care of (along with the children and the house), especially the valuable ones. Notes taped to pots indicating "WATER" or "NO WATER," along with any special directions, is a great suggestion someone once gave me.

HOUSE-SITTING UNDER CONTROL

Yes, you really are responsible for the house (in addition to the children), but if you complete the lists of household information included in this chapter, you will be well-prepared.

When I first began doing extended babysitting, it would be the house problems, and not knowing how to fix them, that would bring tears of frustration to my eyes. Now that I finally know the essential information about my grandchildren's house, I feel very much more at home there, and I am able to deal with whatever comes along.

My panic button doesn't get stuck on HIGH these days. It runs on LOW sometimes, but not on HIGH, like before.

Happy house-sitting!

12

ONE-NIGHT STANDS

As a grandmother do I accept one-night babysitting jobs? Of course not! One-night jobs are for teenagers. Besides, my grandchildren live 1,000 miles away. It just wouldn't happen. But then again, it *could* happen!

Several years ago, my daughter and son-in-law called one afternoon in January. Could I come *tomorrow* to babysit for ten days? My son-in-law's partner was supposed to go with him on an important business trip, but was ill and couldn't travel. My daughter was going to replace the partner and go with my son-in-law, and they needed me right away to care for their two small children.

I bought an airline ticket for the next day to fly from Virginia to Minnesota; but an ice storm was forcing my airport to close until evening. Fortunately that evening, I was able to get one of the last flights to an alternative airport and then make connections to Minnesota, and my daughter and son-in-law were able to catch their plane for the business trip the next day.

But what if I could not have gotten there in time? The grandchildren were just two and six at the time and needed an adult with them. Even the best-laid plans can go astray when bad weather interferes.

Let's say that the daughter in this case is not mine, but is the daughter of some best friends who live a good distance away. Let's say this daughter is someone you knew as a little girl, and now she lives in your area with her husband and children. If she and her husband needed to take this business trip, and the grandparents had a travel snafu, who would be the logical person to call for temporary babysitting help? You, of course.

Oh great, you think. You don't really know the children that well, and you certainly don't know their routines and dietary needs. But the young couple knows and trusts you, and they know that their children will be in good hands until the grandparents arrive.

This is a relatively simple example, with the parents just leaving town for a trip and the grandparents' arrival delayed. But it could be much more serious, with some sort of a medical emergency for one or both of the parents. The situation could involve a neighbor family or friends who live nearby. The important thing to remember is that you are a trusted person and your being there will save the day.

If you are asked to babysit in such a situation, right off state one of the things you will *not* do, which is to take people to and from the airport. The departing and arriving parents and grandparents can take taxis. You need to simplify things as much as possible and focus your attention on the children.

If there is time, and if the children are four or five or older, it is always fun to get them some new crayons and drawing paper (white and multicolored) and/or coloring books for them. Be sure the crayons are age-appropriate—thick crayons for the young children and thin crayons or drawing pens for the older children. If you buy coloring books, make sure they are age-appropriate as well. Books for younger children have simple pictures with dark, thick lines. Each child should have his own set of crayons/pens and coloring books. Just for good measure, get a glue stick, too. It is always fun to make cut-and-glue pictures. Children also like sticker and paint-with-water books. If the children are younger than four, perhaps you could find a small stuffed toy for each child.

You'll probably be able to buy some or all of these things at the grocery store or pharmacy, and large discount stores usually have quite a selection of interesting activities. These gifts are not essential, but they certainly divert the children's attention for a bit. The aim is to arrive at the house with a few surprises that will keep the children happy while you make emergency plans with the parents. Remember, the children are dealing with a difficult situation: their parents are going away, and their grandparents won't be there as planned. In such an emergency situation, a few pleasant diversions will pay off in the long run.

When it comes to "one-night-stand" babysitting you need the primary SOS information about the children prior to the parents' departure. Complete this list (on pages 118–120) with the mother or father either over the phone or in person.

If the children are babies and preschoolers, it is essential that you know exactly what they eat and when. Is there sufficient formula and baby food for the infant? If this is a planned trip, you can assume that the parents have stocked all the provisions and written all the necessary information down for the incoming grandparents. However, if this is an emergency, make sure that you ask about these things—you may have to pick up the special baby food and formula on your way to the house.

If the children are in grade school and older, the food issue is much easier to handle. But it is still imperative to ask if the children are allergic/sensitive to any kind of food. You might think, "Oh well, I'll just fix peanut butter and jelly sandwiches. Kids always like that." Wrong! Any number of children are allergic to peanuts, and sometimes the jelly is too much sugar for the child.

Next on the list of necessary information are school and community-related activities. And last in the hierarchy of concerns is household information. If something goes wrong with the house, call your own repair person, or if it is not an emergency, let the incoming grandparents deal with it. If the house should lose heat in the middle of winter, or air conditioning in the summer, or water or electricity, go next door to the neighbors or take the children to your home. In short-term babysitting situations you aren't responsible for fixing all the problems. Just pay close attention to the children and take care of their needs.

Listed at the end of this chapter is the primary SOS information that you need from the parents. Having the primary SOS information will be a major help to the incoming grandparents, since they won't have any overlap time with the parents. The food, school, community, and house checklists are in the Appendices. If you have time, complete these lists too, since this will be a big help to the grandparents.

If you are sure that you will be babysitting only for one night, and that the parents will be home the next day, it wouldn't be necessary to complete all of the emergency information. Just be prepared for that one night.

On the other hand, if there is an emergency that is not easily re-solved, you might need to stay with the children longer than anticipated. Your "one-night-stand" could turn into an extended babysitting situation. If this does happen, use the additional checklists to gather the information that you'll need in order to be fully prepared.

Remember, whether this is a "one-night-stand" or an extended babysitting stint, you are a trusted person and you will save the day just by being there.

The parents have chosen you because they feel you are a very responsible person who will be warm and friendly with their children. They also feel you are flexible enough to adjust quickly to whatever needs to be done. It is a great compliment that the parents turned to you in their time of need.

EMERGENCY SOS INFORMATION
(For One-Night Stand)

Parents' hotel name _____

Hotel phone _____

Parents' pager number _____

Parents' cell phone number _____

Doctor's name _____

Doctor's phone _____

Doctor's address _____

Hospital name _____

Hospital phone _____

Hospital address _____

Pharmacy name _____

Pharmacy phone _____

Pharmacy address _____

Poison control center _____

Poison control phone _____

Emergency: 911

Dentist's name _____

Dentist's phone _____

Dentist's address _____

Veterinarian's name _____

Veterinarian's phone _____

Veterinarian's address _____

HEALTH INFORMATION
(For One-Night Stand)

Location of health-care cards _____
_____

Location of prescription medicines _____
_____

Location of nonprescription medicines _____
_____

Dosages of medicines _____
_____

Any allergies? Who? To what? List all food/environmental allergies: _____

_____

LETTER OF PERMISSION
(One-Night Stand)

Written and signed ? _____

Where is it? _____

Below is a format you might use:

(Your name) _____ has full responsibility for my children, (give names) _____, _____,

_____, _____,

from (starting date) _____ until (ending date) _____.
This includes seeking emergency medical and dental care and dealing with all school-related issues.
Parent(s) name(s) _____

_____ Date_____

Remember, this letter only covers you for the brief time that you are in charge. Be sure that the parents write an identical letter to cover the grandparents or other adult caretakers who are on their way. When the caretaker adults arrive, put their letter of permission in their hands and explain what it is. Don't let it get lost in all the confusion.

13

HOME AGAIN, HOME AGAIN

Ahhhh . . . the parents have returned home, the gifts and stories have been shared, and at last it is time for Grandpa and Grandma to go home. As much as we have enjoyed spending time with our grandchildren and seeing our daughter and son-in-law again, we are eager to get home to familiar surroundings and relax.

Almost inevitably, however, upon returning home one or both of us is suffering from a sore throat, a severe head cold, or some vague illness. We are very healthy people, but given the many opportunities we've had for exposure to germs new to us—such as traveling on an airplane and living with grandchildren who are exposed to a variety of illnesses in school—it's no wonder that we bring something back with us.

Unfortunately, it has happened so consistently to us that we are now very careful not to schedule other major events too close to our return. In recent years we have had to cancel some special events that were scheduled immediately after returning from babysitting our grandchildren.

Remember what my friend said after babysitting twin baby granddaughters? "We be old." We aren't as young as we were when we were raising our own children. While I'm babysitting, I go at a fast, steady pace. When I finally get home, I make sure that I have time to go at a very *slow* pace. I've discovered that many other grandparents also try to schedule a very *slow* time after an extended babysitting stint.

Be good to yourself! You have given your children a major gift by babysitting your grandchildren. Now it is time to relax. After all, the travel section of the newspaper is showing some very exciting places to explore. A new adventure is just around the corner. Catch your breath and get going.

For those of you who have no grandchildren of your own, but just finished babysitting for friends and relatives, consider what a wonderful gift you have given—your time, interest, warmth, humor, and energy!

I hope that following the guidelines of *A Grandmother's Guide to Extended Babysitting* helped you to relax and enjoy your time with the children. If so, there will always be a next time!

Happy Babysitting!

APPENDICES

THINGS I WANT TO REMEMBER TO PACK

_____
_____
_____
_____
_____
_____
_____

PARENTS' AND CHILDREN'S WISH LIST

_____
_____
_____
_____
_____
_____

INFANTS' AND PRESCHOOLERS' ROUTINES

You must know the following specifics:

What formula to use (warm or cool) _____

When to feed the baby _____

What solid food the baby can eat _____

What the preschooler eats _____

When the preschooler eats _____

Foods *not* to give the child _____

Where the diapers are kept _____

The sleeping schedules _____

If and when the baby uses a pacifier _____

Rules about infant/toddler traveling in a car _____

The location and use of the car seat _____

The location of the baby carriage or stroller _____

The location of jackets/sweaters/hats _____

_____

_____

MEALTIME CHORES

Who helps prepare the meal? _____

Who sets the table? _____

How is the table cleared of dirty dishes? _____

Who washes dishes or loads the dishwasher? _____

Who empties the dishwasher? _____

Who puts out the garbage? _____

Who does other kitchen-related jobs? _____

OTHER MEALTIME CHORES

_____

_____

_____

_____

_____

_____

_____

A.M. ROUTINES

You need to know the following information:

Wake-up time _____

Dressing routines (Does anyone need help with clothes or hair?)

_____

Breakfast time _____

Who packs lunches _____

Lunch money amount _____

Departure times _____

School bus schedule _____

Bus numbers _____

Additional reminders _____

_____

_____

_____

AFTERNOON ROUTINES

Schedules and routines that you need to know:

After-school arrival home _____

_____

Where do the books and homework go? _____

After-school activities (times and places) _____

_____

_____

_____

Homework (time and place) _____

Dinnertime _____

Chore times _____

_____

_____

BEDTIME ROUTINES

Nightly checklist:

Pack books and homework in backpacks _____

Place the backpacks next to the exit door _____

Place hat, jackets, boots, sweaters, umbrellas (as needed) next to exit door _____

Lay out clothes for next day _____

Bath time _____

Who needs help with the bath? _____

Who does the hair washing? _____

Brush teeth _____

Put on pajamas _____

"Icing on the cake" details:

What do the children like best? (back rubs, songs, stories read, hugs, kisses, etc.) _____

Describe other bedtime routines _____

_____

_____

GRANDCHILDREN'S CHORE LIST

Name _____

Chores _____

_____

_____

Name _____

Chores _____

_____

Name _____

Chores _____

_____

Name _____

Chores _____

_____

PET PARTICULARS

If there's a pet in the picture, this is the information you need to know:

Who feeds the pet(s)? _____

Who walks the dog? _____

Where is the leash kept? _____

Who changes the cat's litter box? _____ How often? _____

Where does the pet sleep? _____

May the pet be outside? _____

Other duties, details, and routines: _____

_____

_____

_____

_____

_____

THE DIRT ON THE LAUNDRY

Laundry information you probably should know:

Where is the dirty laundry basket kept? _____

Is each child responsible for putting his dirty laundry in that basket? _____

Which children do their own laundry and when? _____

Any special operating instructions for the washer and/or dryer? _____

When can we have the clothes-folding party? _____

Is ironing expected? _____

Other laundry and clothes instructions: _____

_____

_____

GRANDMA'S PLANNER

Scheduled events you should know about:

Athletic practice/events _____

_____

Other activities/events _____

_____

Scout meetings _____

_____

Weekly appointments for physical/speech therapy _____

_____

Doctor appointments _____

Dentist appointments _____

Orthodontist appointments _____

Other appointments _____

_____

_____

GRANDMA'S MAILBOX

How are you going to deal with:

Field trip permission slips to be signed? _____

A note from a teacher requiring your signature? _____

Homework/test papers to be signed? _____

Other important mystery papers that need your attention? _____

Phone or other messages? _____

_____

_____

FRIENDS

Here are issues that should be addressed:

When are the children allowed to socialize with friends? _____

Which friends are okay for them to socialize with? _____

Friend's phone _____ address _____

Friend's phone _____ address _____

Any friend on the "NO" list? _____

"NO" list friend's phone _____ address _____

Whose house is off-limits? _____

Is the child allowed to go "mall walking" with friends? _____

Does the teenager have permission to drive in the parent's absence? _____

Can he/she ride with other teen drivers? _____

Is there a curfew on school nights or weekends? ____ Time? ____

Are dates allowed? ____ What are rules concerning dates? ____

What places are the children not allowed to visit? _____

SLEEPOVERS

The rules for sleepovers:

Are they allowed? No _____Yes _____

At grandchildren's house? No _____Yes _____

At friend's house? No _____Yes _____

Is one planned at a friend's house during my visit? _____

Friend's name _____ phone _____

Address/directions _____

_____

Date/time of sleepover _____

_____

What else do I need to know? _____

_____

NIGHTTIME ACTIVITIES

Essential nighttime activities: _____

_____

Possible nighttime activities : _____

_____

Nighttime activities on the "NO" list: _____

_____

_____

CLOTHES

Clothes that may *not* be worn to school:

_____

_____

_____

TELEPHONE

Rules for phone use:

When _____

How long _____

Other phone restrictions _____

Does the teen have a cell phone? What is the number? _____

TELEVISION

Learn the parental rules for television, including:

How often may the children watch TV? _____

How long? _____

When? _____

What programs are allowed? _____

What programs are not allowed? _____

Which channels are allowed? _____

Which ones are forbidden? _____

How close can they sit? _____

HOMEWORK

The rules for homework:

When _____

Where _____

How long _____

Music, TV, phone calls allowed during homework time?

Yes _____No _____

COMPUTERS

In this computer age the concerns are:

Is there a computer designated for parents only that is not to be used by the children? _____

Where? _____

Is there a computer for the grandchildren to use? _____

Where? _____

When may the children use the computer? _____
_____

For how long? _____
_____

What software applications/programs are they allowed to use?
_____

What software applications/programs aren't they allowed to use?
_____

Are they allowed to go on the Internet? _____

What are their limitations regarding Internet surfing? _____

Other information: _____

ALLOWANCE

Allowances for each child:

Child _____ amount _____

Child _____ amount _____

Child _____ amount _____

Child _____ amount _____

When paid? _____

Requirements/stipulations _____

Spending restrictions? _____

ATHLETIC EQUIPMENT

Locations for storing athletic equipment:

Bikes _____ Bike tire pump _____
Helmets _____ Shin guards _____
Baseball, bat, ball, glove _____
Football _____ Basketball _____ Soccer ball _____
Inline skates _____
Ice skates _____ Hockey stick, puck _____
Skis, poles _____ Boots _____
Snow board _____ Boots _____
Bathing suits _____ Surfboard _____
Boogie board _____ Snorkel, fins, goggles _____
Other _____

Sports rules:

Where can kids skate or ride bikes? _____
Can they go alone? _____

Do they need supervision or assistance with:

Biking? _____
Skating? _____
Swimming? _____

PARKS AND PLAYGROUNDS

If the grandchildren are older (grade-school age), find out the family rules regarding parks and playgrounds.

May they walk there? _____

May they ride their bikes there? _____

Do you need to drive them? _____

Park _____

Location/directions _____

_____

Playground _____

Location/directions _____

_____

HIDDEN FOOD ALLERGIES/SENSITIVITIES

Hidden food allergies or sensitivities in a child might manifest themselves in the following ways:

Dark circles or "bags" under the eyes _____

Constant sniffling, itchy nose, and clearing of the throat _____

Nervous, irritable, or overactive behavior _____

Tiredness or drowsiness _____

Headaches _____

Stomachaches _____

Frequent respiratory problems _____

Chronic colds and ear infections _____

Digestive problems _____

What health concerns do you have about your grandchild?

_____

_____

POSSIBLE PROBLEM FOOD PRODUCTS

High on the list are products containing:

Wheat _____

Dairy products _____

Corn _____

Sugar _____

Artificial coloring and additives _____

Chocolate _____

Eggs _____

Peanuts _____

Citrus _____

FAVORITE PLACES TO GO

_____

_____

_____

_____

_____

_____

_____

FAVORITE THINGS TO DO

_____

_____

_____

_____

_____

_____

_____

FAVORITE RESTAURANTS

_____
_____
_____
_____
_____
_____
_____
_____

SPECIAL PROJECTS TO DO

_____
_____
_____
_____
_____
_____
_____
_____

SPECIAL BOOKS TO READ

_____
_____
_____
_____
_____
_____
_____
_____

LETTER OF PERMISSION

The "letter of permission" says that you have full responsibility for the children for a specific length of time. Here is a format you might use:

(Your name) _____ has full responsibility for my children, (give names)_____,_____,_____,
_____, from (starting date) _____ until (ending date)_____.
This includes seeking medical and dental care and dealing with all school-related issues.

Parent(s) name(s) _____

Signature(s) _____

Date _____

PARENTS' ITINERARY

Parent contact information:

Hotel name _____

Hotel address _____

Hotel phone number _____

Parent's pager number _____

Parent's cell phone number _____

Date of departure _____

Date of return _____

Airline _____

Flight number and departure time _____

Flight number and return time _____

Who is responsible for parents' transportation to and from the airport? _____

HEALTH CARE DOCUMENTS

As soon as possible, locate the following items for each child and put them with the letter of permission:

Health Insurance/HMO identity card _____

Rx card _____

Medical ID card _____

Clinic card _____

Military dependent ID card _____

Other identity cards _____

HOME HEALTH CARE

Medication information that you need:

Age and weight of each child (dosage is often determined by weight) _____

Prescription medicines and locations _____

Who gets which prescription medicine? _____

When is the prescription medicine given? _____

What over-the-counter medicine for headache? _____

What over-the-counter medicine for temperature? _____

What over-the-counter medicine for tummyache? _____

What over-the-counter medicine for cough? _____

Who is allergic to what medicine? _____

Who is allergic to what foods? _____

Where is the small humidifier kept? _____

Where are the cough drops kept? _____

Where are the thermometer and first aid kit kept? _____

Do any of the children have any chronic or recurring illnesses (asthma, croup, ear infections)? _____

How should these be treated? _____

PROFESSIONAL HEALTH CARE

Essential information:

Doctor _____

Doctor's phone _____

Doctor's address _____

Directions _____
_____

Hospital name _____

Hospital phone _____

Hospital address _____

Directions _____
_____

Pharmacy _____

Pharmacy phone _____

Pharmacy address _____

Directions _____
_____

Poison control center _____

Poison control center phone _____

Emergency-911

Fire department phone _____

Police department phone _____

Dentist _____

Dentist's phone _____

Dentist's address _____

Directions _____
_____

Additional medical emergency information _____
_____

LETTER OF PERMISSION FOR PETS

Below is a format you might use:

(Your name) _____has full responsibility for my dog(s) or cat(s), (give names) _____, _____, _____, from (starting date) _____, until (ending date) _____.
This includes seeking emergency medical care. I do want to be informed immediately, however, so that I may decide the length and depth of medical care that is appropriate and the costs that might be incurred.
Pet owner's name _____,
Date signed _____,

EMERGENCY INFORMATION FOR PETS

Veterinarian _____

Veterinarian's phone _____

Veterinarian's address _____

_____

Directions _____

_____

Does the pet have any health problems? _____

_____

Other information: _____

_____

_____

_____

_____

SCHOOL DIRECTORY

School information that you need for each child:

Child _____

School name _____ phone _____

School address _____

Teacher's name _____

Child _____

School name _____ phone _____

School address _____

Teacher's name _____

Child _____

School name _____ phone _____

School address _____ phone _____

Teacher's name _____

Directions to schools: _____

_____

_____

_____

AFTER-SCHOOL PROGRAMS

After-school information that you need to know:

Daycare center name _____ phone _____

Daycare center address _____

End-of-day pickup time _____

Directions _____

_____

_____

_____

NEIGHBORS

Important "helpful neighbor" information:

Name _____

Phone number _____

Address _____

_____

_____

Other information _____

_____

_____

Name _____

Phone number _____

Address _____

_____

_____

Other information _____

_____

_____

Name _____

Phone number _____

Address _____

_____

_____

Other information _____

_____

_____

COMMUNITY CONTACTS

Sports coach _____ phone _____

Practice athletic field address/directions _____

_____

_____

Scout leader _____ phone _____

Meeting place address/directions _____

_____

_____

Parents of friends _____ phone _____

Meeting place address/directions _____

_____

_____

Parents of friends _____ phone _____

Meeting place address/directions _____

_____

_____

Parents of friends _____ phone _____

Meeting place address/directions _____

_____

_____

Additional community person _____ phone _____

Additional community person _____ phone _____

KEYS

Locations of keys for:

House _____

Car _____

All other vehicles _____

Storage areas _____

Garage _____

Bike locks _____

Other _____

_____

Special instructions regarding locks _____

_____

Information on car or house alarm systems _____

_____

DOES ANYONE KNOW A GOOD . . . ?

You'll need the names and numbers of a plumber, electrician, and a heating company.

Information you should have (and hopefully won't need):

Plumber _____

Plumber's phone _____

Electrician _____

Electrician's phone _____

Heating/furnace company _____

Heating company's phone _____

Appliance repair shop _____

List the locations of the:

Thermostat(s) _____

Fuse boxes _____

Main water connection _____

Water meter _____

Alarm system (codes, passwords, how to operate it) _____

Flashlights (that work) and extra batteries _____

Basic tools (including a variety of screwdrivers) _____

That very important plunger for the toilet _____

Lightbulbs _____

Matches and candles _____

Other house quirks you should know about (such as any plugs or appliances that you shouldn't use because they'll blow the circuits) _____

It would be very helpful to know the location of the instructions for operating the myriad of appliances in the house, including:

TV/VCR _____

CD/Tape player _____

Microwave _____

Garbage disposal _____

Washer _____

Dryer _____

Other _____

_____

_____

_____

GARBAGE

Garbage collection information:

Day(s) _____

Time _____

Recycling _____

Other information _____

SNOW SHOVELS, BROOMS, SEASONAL EQUIPMENT

List the locations of:

Snow shovel _____

Good broom _____

Scraper for ice/snow on the car _____

WHERE IN THE WORLD AM I? OR WHO'S GOT A MAP?

Street locations to mark on your map:

House _____

Schools _____

Playgrounds _____

Athletic fields _____

Grocery stores _____

Hospital _____

Doctor _____

Dentist _____

Veterinarian _____

Pharmacy _____

EMERGENCY SOS INFORMATION
(For One-Night Stand)

Parents' hotel name _____

Hotel phone _____

Parents' pager number _____

Parents' cell phone number _____

Doctor's name _____

Doctor's phone _____

Doctor's address _____

Hospital name _____

Hospital phone _____

Hospital address _____

Pharmacy name _____

Pharmacy phone _____

Pharmacy address _____

Poison control center _____

Poison control phone _____

Emergency: 911

Dentist's name _____

Dentist's phone _____

Dentist's address _____

Veterinarian's name _____

Veterinarian's phone _____

Veterinarian's address _____

HEALTH INFORMATION (SHORT FORM)
(For One-Night Stand)

Location of health-care cards _____

_____

Location of prescription medicines _____

_____

Location of nonprescription medicines _____

_____

Dosages of medicines _____

_____

Any allergies? Who? To what? List all food/environmental
allergies: _____

_____

LETTER OF PERMISSION
(For One-Night Stand)

Written and signed? _____
Where is it? _____

Below is a format you might use:

(Your name) _____ has full responsibility for my
children, (give names) _____, _____
_____, _____, _____ from
(starting date) _____, until (ending date) _____.
This includes taking them for all emergency medical, dental and
school care they need.
Parent(s) name(s) _____
_____Date _____

Now this only covers you for the brief time that you are there. While you
are having this letter written, have the parents write an identical letter to

cover the grandparents or other adult caretakers who are on their way. When the caretaker adults arrive, put their letter of permission in their hands and explain what it is. Don't let it get lost in all the confusion.

RECIPE INDEX